EVERY TIME I SAY

I SAY

Grace,

We FIGHT

SANDRA FINLEY DORAN

EVERY TIME I SAY Grace, We FiGHT

Practical help for marriages divided by religion but united by love

REVIEW AND HERALD® PUBLISHING ASSOCIATION
HAGERSTOWN, MD 21740

The author assumes full responsibility for the accuracy of all facts and
quotations as cited in this book.

Texts credited to NIV are from the *Holy Bible, New International Version.*
Copyright © 1973, 1978, International Bible Society. Used by permission
of Zondervan Bible Publishers.

Bible texts credited to RSV are from the Revised Standard Version of the
Bible, copyright 1946, 1952 © 1971, 1973.

This book was
Edited by Richard W. Coffen
Designed by Ron J. Pride
Cover Photo: Joel D. Springer
Type set: 11.7/12.7 Zapf Book Light

PRINTED IN U.S.A.

98 97 96 95 94 93 92   10 9 8 7 6 5 4 3 2 1

R&H Cataloging Service
   Every time I say grace, we fight.

      1. Intermarriage, Religious. I. Title.
              301.42

ISBN 0-8280-0645-8

To Eric

who prodded printers that refused to stay on-line
and fought with sheafs of perforated pages,
delivering me from being forever hopelessly
entrapped in a paper jam,
I lovingly dedicate this book.

Contents

Author's Note

I grew up in a home with a Catholic mother and a Protestant father. Through the respect they showed one another, I witnessed a love that transcended all barriers.

Now, as the wife of a gospel minister, reaching out to couples struggling with the issue of religion in the family, I think often of the powerful message instilled in me during my younger years. My mind goes back to a blue ranch on Lucas Park Road; to my Protestant father, who faithfully drove his children to catechism each week; and to my Catholic mother, who sent her daughters to Vacation Bible School.

The lessons I learned as a child were not those of divisiveness, mistrust, and hate, but rather those of creative solutions, tolerance, and love.

I am grateful for the acceptance and understanding I have been given for those of all faiths and all levels of understanding. Recalling fondly the model of my childhood home, I am filled with a spirit of optimism for all couples striving to make a cohesive family unit of religiously separate and distinct individuals.

February 25, 1991

Introduction

"My husband and I have such different values. I chose not to have a drink on the first night of our vacation this year, and it literally ruined the whole trip. The old argument over religion was brought up again, and we trooped around Disneyland like one dejected family."

♦♦♦♦♦♦

"My wife and I come from totally different backgrounds—I'm Jewish and she's Protestant. When we got married, both sets of parents clamored for a religious service. We finally ended up disappointing everybody by having just a civil ceremony."

♦♦♦♦♦♦

"I think my husband knows the only reason I'm staying with him is because I know how much he hates divorce. To be honest, I would be relieved to find that my husband has been cheating on me. Then, at least, I'd have a biblical reason to leave him."

♦♦♦♦♦♦

"I should have known religion would become a dividing point in our marriage when my future mother-in-law called me aside before the wedding and made disparaging remarks about my religion. As it turned out, Dave's parents ruled our home by their strong influence on Dave's thinking. Dave himself was never overtly religious, yet when our children came along he insisted that they be raised in the same religious tradition he had been taught as a child. He was horrified when I suggested sending the boys to the school sponsored by my church. And that was just the beginning of our problems."

♦♦♦♦♦♦

"Religion has always been a source of contention in our home. I've tried for so long to open up to my husband . . . but it's not worth it. So I just keep everything to myself now."

The comments come from neighbors, coworkers, members of my congregation. "I'm working on a manuscript about religion in marriage," I casually mention, and the stories come tumbling out.

It is not easy, marching to the beat of opposite drummers day after day, year after year. The issues are complex. How does a Christian respond to the insistent tugs of church, home, and an unbelieving mate? How does a nonbeliever put up with the constant demands on a spouse's time—the never-ending prayer meetings, board meetings, services, and luncheons—without feeling like an "outsider"? And what about two seriously committed, responsibly religious individuals whose commitments run in opposite directions? Is it possible for them to continue their own spiritual allegiances and still maintain a high level of respect for each other? And what of child-raising, goal-setting, weekends, and holidays?

Answers do not come easily. There are no formulas, magic steps, or lines to memorize that automatically ease the stress and set the environment back into balance. Yet through insight comes understanding; through understanding, tolerance; and through tolerance, acceptance. As you read this book, take a look at some of the common mistakes others are making in their approach to marriage with individuals whose religious beliefs do not parallel their own. Contrast these stories with those of couples who are struggling to find answers. And then, in the context of your own marriage, begin the process of making your relationship work—despite the differences.

Communication:
The Tools of the Trade

1

Wouldn't it be easy if open communication were a "given" in every marriage—handed to us on our wedding day along with the marriage license and carload of gifts?

Why is it so hard, sometimes, to put aside all barriers and share what we are really thinking and feeling? Could it be that we fear opening ourselves up is too dangerous—too potentially damaging to our own self-esteem? The possibility always exists that we will be rejected, judged, criticized. Even within our own marriages.

A friend of mine recently shared some views on communication in marriage that I suspect represent what many today are feeling yet are often afraid to voice.

"I really want to make my wife happy," Frank confided. "And I feel that I do hold similar religious convictions, yet there are some things that I just can't seem to get a handle on.

"Like smoking, for example. I know it upsets Jean to see me smoke. And the church frowns on it. So when I feel a need to light up, I find myself trying to hide it. Like making some lame excuse about going out for a cup of coffee.

"Then I feel like such a failure. . . . I hate having to cover up the whole thing, yet I know that if Jean finds out, she'll became hurt and upset. So I live my life like some stupid little kid, hiding behind the barn every time I want a smoke."

Frank is obviously torn—between a habit he can't seem to break and the expectations his wife holds for his conduct. In further explaining his dilemma, Frank related that he is concerned about the hazards of smoking and has tried to stop, yet he always seems to revert to his old habit. And the more he smokes, the more he withdraws from his wife, knowing that honest communication will bring only her disapproval, disappointment, disdain.

We shun communication because it does not always appear to be worth the effort. If we don't talk, we spare ourselves the risk of vulnerability.

I will never forget one of the first pastoral visits I made with my husband, early in our ministry. As we chatted pleasantly with a member of our church—a woman in her 80s—she casually mentioned that her husband, Bob, had fled to the basement as soon as he heard our car pull into the driveway. "He always goes down there when a preacher comes to call," she explained. "He tells me he's guarding his whiskey—in case a pastor be tempted to take off with some of it!"

As our ministry in that parish continued, we discovered more about Bob. He wanted nothing to do with his wife's religion and refused even to discuss the topic of God. Communication was almost nonexistent.

What had led up to such apparent hostility? Bob's emotional wounds were deep. As a child he felt rejected by his parents and sought desperately for peer approval. Then one day, in the midst of his teen years, an altar call at his church deeply moved him. Almost without thinking he rose from his seat, making his way to the front of the church. But he never got there. A classmate extended a foot into the aisle, and much laughter over Bob's plight erupted from a particular row of boys. Thereafter he experienced alienation and scorn, never feeling part of the group again.

At that point in Bob's life, the topic of religion became a closed subject. Sixty years later communication was no easier.

Bob's story is rather extreme, yet all of us find ourselves at times doing anything but sharing our true feelings and ideas. A new Christian admitted to me once, "I'm afraid to be open, to let my husband know how I really feel, because if I do, he may see that I'm not as kind as I ought to be, or as sweet as my Christianity should lead me to be. My real fear, I guess, is that he'll see right through me—consider me to be a hypocrite—and then there'll be no chance of his accepting my church's beliefs."

Mary's fear is not surprising, considering the counsel often given to those who are "unequally yoked." The popular advice to the believing spouse is: "Don't preach it; live it. Be as kind as you possibly can be; do everything you can to show your spouse the power Christianity has in your life."

There's nothing wrong with such advice in and of itself. However, it often brings a load of guilt, pressure, and even dishonesty to the relationship. Linda Davis, in her book *How to Be the Happy Wife of an Unsaved Husband*, brings out this point with a series of questions: "How often do you catch yourself thinking, *If only I were doing certain things better—loving, submitting, witnessing—he would already be a born-again wonder?* Do you ever feel like he won't accept Christ because your failures and imperfections are a stumbling block? If I hadn't been so crabby the other day? *If I weren't always yelling at the kids? If I hadn't run up the charge account?* Do you ever blame yourself?" [1]

The bottom line is that in order to make a relationship—any relationship—work, we have to make ourselves vulnerable. Any falseness, any holding up of an image for the image's sake, will not work. Communication will break down, and the quality of the relationship will be forfeited. With two individuals who do not share the same religious beliefs, a strong communication pattern is vital to survival.

What are the basics of communication? In conducting communication seminars, I have discovered that many people view the subject strictly in terms of getting their own points across. They want to learn how to *communicate*—how to send their own messages in no uncertain terms—and so they attend my seminars. Yet the vital key that keeps communication alive in a marriage is attentive *listening*.

And listening, contrary to popular belief, is not passive but very active. As your spouse presents his or her point, you are listening through the "filter" of your own perceptual set. All your background, previous experience, and personal insights come into play as you attempt to sort out just exactly what is being said. As you respond to these messages, revealing your perception of his or her words, your spouse is able to clarify the point or points at issue.

Let me put this in very simple terms by referring to a couple who illustrate the point clearly.

Diane grew up as an only child in a very peaceful home. Her father was often away on trips, and her mother, a full-time homemaker, spoke only in quiet, gentle tones. On the other hand, Diane's husband, Louis, was raised as part of a boisterous family of four boys. In his home, the order of the day was simply put: "If you want something, make yourself heard."

During the early days of their marriage, Diane and Louis experienced quite a bit of conflict over Louis's loud and aggressive manner of getting a point across. Filtered through the perceptual set of Diane's sheltered background, every comment sounded like ammunition for an argument, every opinion an overstatement. Gradually, however, through the process of communication, Diane and Louis were able to sort through their individual perceptions and backgrounds to discover the true intent of their messages to each other. By providing Louis with feedback on how she was perceiving his messages, Diane enabled him to clarify the points he was attempting to make.

And just as a difference in backgrounds can make communication a real challenge, so the dichotomy between male and female communication patterns adds an even more interesting element to the whole process. In a marriage in which religion appears to be a stress point, couples often blame their troubles on the difference in religion, when in reality the source of the problem might be more closely related to a basic difference of communication style.

There are three basic areas in which men and women generally approach the language differently.[2]

How many women do you know who complain that their husbands don't listen to them? Or maybe you feel that way yourself. Interestingly enough, research has shown that men simply do not give the same type of signals that women do to *show* that they are listening. When a man is listening, he might be concentrating very intently on what his wife is saying, but he is not always nodding at appropriate points, smiling, or vocalizing with "Uh-huh," "Yeah," or "I see what you mean." And his wife feels that she is not being heard. While a woman interprets a man's lack of verbal responsiveness to indicate uninterest, it might simply reflect a differing communication style.

Another area that pokes a potential pin into the bubble of marital communication is the manner in which men and women approach a subject. Women generally introduce a topic with the goal of discussing all the ramifications and reaching a mutual conclusion, but men often view conversation in terms of black-and-white. As a result, when a woman brings up a topic hoping to negotiate, a man often misses the cue and answers her question on a strictly informational level.

For example, Betty wishes to redecorate the bedroom and asks her husband, George, what color he feels they ought to paint the walls.

"Light blue."

"I was thinking more along the lines of a mint green," she responds.

Puzzled, he asks, "Then why did you ask me?"

Betty was attempting to open the floor for discussion: "What color would you like to paint the bedroom?"

"How about blue?"

"Yes, blue would be nice, but I kind of prefer green."

"Are you sure you wouldn't get tired of green after a while?"

"No, I really think I'd be happy with green, but if blue is your preference . . ."

"No, I don't have strong feelings on the matter. Green is fine."

George, on the other hand, took Betty's question at face value—a query as to his personal preference.

Such a scenario is reenacted in marriages all the time. I don't know how many people have expressed relief when I've shared this communication principle with them. "Oh, then you mean we're 'normal'?" Indeed!

The third area of communication difference between the sexes involves the role of language as it relates to intimacy. As an elementary school teacher, I've had many opportunities to observe firsthand this difference of style. Little girls, as they play together, love to tell secrets, whisper confidences. The glue that cements friendship for girls is the shared language— the words that define their world. Boys, on the other hand, are happy to *do* things together. It is generally not as important for a boy to *tell* all his secrets to a friend, as it is for him to run a truck along the floor beside him, throw him a ball, hike the same trail.

And as adults, we tend to retain the same needs as they relate to language. For women, intimacy is tied in to the pleasant exchange of personal details, the reliving of events through words, the shared commentaries. Research shows that men, on the average, tend to be content with shared experiences—whether language is involved or not.

In a marriage in which so many things can lead to conflict because of a different perspective on religion, it is crucial to recognize and appreciate these basic differences of communication style, lest they serve as yet more fuel added to the fire of religious wars.

And such differences of communication style between men and women are not the only variations that can cause tension in a marriage. Tim LaHaye, in his book *How to Be Happy Though Married*, outlines four basic personality types that are present in greater or lesser degrees in individuals. Such varied temperaments can also account for "communication blocks" between individuals when two people think, relate, or feel on totally different planes.

Whether you are an outgoing *sanguine*, who can talk to anybody about anything, or an introspective *melancholy*, who prefers to work alone over a piece on the piano, you have your own way of approaching life. And more than likely, your spouse has an altogether different personality type. Those who love making "To Do" checklists often find themselves married to those who can't remember the day's appointments. And the calmer, cool, collected *phlegmatic* often finds himself married to a *choleric*, who will laugh or cry at the drop of a hat.

The important thing to recognize is that each temperament has both positive and negative aspects. No one way of relating to life is "right" or "wrong." And the more you understand what makes your spouse tick, what kinds of things motivate him or her to do and say the things that he or she does, the more you are headed toward mutual understanding and respect.

It is important, even vital, to step out of your own limited perspective and established way of looking at things and try to see things through your spouse's eyes, experience situations as he or she might experience them. It is often easy for us to find a logical reason that our spouse should behave in a manner that makes perfect sense to us. But our logic does not always provide us with a window into the feelings and life experiences of another.

Emotions are very real and not always subdued by reason and principle in the way that we would like them to be. And the first step toward establishing a strong relationship of any type is to communicate our feelings, open up the deepest stirrings of our heart, make ourselves vulnerable to each other. This in turn will give the other the confidence to do the same.

If you consider yourself to be more serious about religion than your spouse, then it is crucial for you to let your spouse know that you are still a *real* person, with real feelings, emotions, heartaches, and triumphs. If you feel that you do not share the same high level of interest in religion as your spouse, it is vital for you to communicate the deepest stirrings of your heart, your interests, concerns, joys, and fears. Thus you will create a bond that will transcend all differences.

Josef Goldbrunner, a psychiatrist noted for his ability to "gain instant access to the deepest parts of anyone within a matter of minutes," says that the key to getting others to open up is not in probing into their areas of insecurity, but in *opening up yourself honestly to them, telling them of your own deepest feelings.*[4]

An important point to remember, however, is that this process of opening up leaves no room for passing judgment on anyone's part. The quickest way to kill an open sharing session is to sit in judgment on a vulnerable soul who is admitting fright, anger, embarrassment, or loneliness.

Admittedly, the whole process of communicating openly and honestly, of daring to make ourselves vulnerable, of stripping off the mask of pretension, is a great risk. Many people hiding behind established roles of "Christian spouse" or "passive partner" are unwilling to take it. Some, like Cathy, a dedicated Christian mother in her early 40s, spend their whole life attempting to shut off emotion, to insulate a fragile ego from pain, and so they find themselves alienated from a life partner, afflicted with headaches and feeling very much alone. Others, like Louis, dare to lower the mask, and step by step through trial and error, joy and sorrow, draw closer to those they love.

Notes

[1] Linda Davis, *How to Be the Happy Wife of an Unsaved Husband* (Pittsburgh: Whitaker House, 1986), p. 9.

[2] These three areas are discussed in detail in an article by Deborah Tannen, "Did You Say What I Just Heard?" Washington *Post*, Oct. 12, 1986.

[3] Tim LaHaye, *How to Be Happy Though Married* (Wheaton, Ill.: Tyndale House, 1968).

[4] John Powell, *Why Am I Afraid to Tell You Who I Am?* (Allen, Tex.: Argus Communications, 1969), p. 84.

Conflict: Dealing With the Differences

2

So you're learning to communicate, to open yourself up to your partner with all honesty and vulnerability. But what happens when the two of you conflict, butt heads on an issue, reach an absolute impasse? Should you press on for a mutual agreement, drop the issue, or attempt to avoid conflict altogether? And what happens when the conflict centers on that most touchy subject of all—religion? Are there kid gloves soft enough to handle *that* issue?

In an article published in *Health* magazine, Dr. Georgia Witkin-Lanoil advises couples with differing religious backgrounds to "talk about 'taboo' topics." "Too often," she states, "couples avoid subjects about which they think they'll disagree. This does not help them avoid stress; it just produces closet conflict and silent misunderstandings." [1]

I was interested recently to find a television talk show featuring marriage partners of different religious backgrounds. TV host Sally Jessy Raphael opened up the topic by making a statement that emphasized the need for open communication right from the start. "If you do not confront the issue of religion early on," she said, "it could become a time bomb that will go off later in the marriage." [2]

Confrontation. Not always a comfortable word. Something we'd rather avoid—especially within our own homes. Yet psychiatrist Alfred B. Messer sees conflict as actually necessary to a healthy marriage. "A spirited spat is good for most marriages," he says. "Those marriages that exist without any type of fighting are generally frozen or inflexible marriages in which other aspects of the relationship are compromised in order to maintain the facade of peace and harmony." [3] But how much verbal battling can fit comfortably into the range of a "spirited spat"? Is there a point at which enough becomes too much?

I can never think about conflict in marriage without bringing to mind Rosa and Allen, a newly married and promising young couple who entered our church several years ago. As the weeks passed, however, it became apparent that something was not right. The couple declined all invitations to dinners, staying uncomfortably in the background. Allen finally stopped by one afternoon and opened up the topic.

"I guess you've been wondering why Rosa and I never want to share a meal with anyone. I'll be honest with you, Pastor. We're afraid to. We argue almost constantly. I don't think we could make it through a meal without embarrassing ourselves and making everyone else feel uncomfortable."

As Allen continued talking, we discovered that he'd met his wife at a church picnic. As a new Christian, he found himself drawn to Rosa, with her solid background and apparent faith. But after the wedding, he discovered that things were not as they ought to be. Conflict began to build. Home became unbearable.

Rosa's background, it turned out, was far from the idyllic picture she had painted for Allen. Born one month before her parents' marriage, Rosa had been looked upon as an embarrassing intrusion for all 20 years of her life. Her mother, an outspoken woman bearing a heavy load of guilt, filled her days by heaping a barrage of harassment upon her husband and daughter; thus Rosa entered her own marriage with a background of strife and bickering as her model. The constant conflict she brought into her new home was too much for the relationship to bear. From the very beginning the marriage began to flounder, and by the third year, divorce papers had been signed.

Conflict. How can it be held to a manageable level— faced squarely yet on a plane above the pettiness of attack/counterattack strategy?

There are certain basics that help keep any discussion between people from becoming spiteful and intimidating. Consider these 10 points the next time you and your spouse have some touchy ground to cover, particularly in the area of religion.

1. Choose your battles.

I remember my father stressing again and again when I was a young girl the point that it is not necessary to make every minor infraction a major cause for war. After a while, if we become noted for taking issue with every minor difference encountered, others do not bother to take us seriously. In a marriage in which religion already offers enough difference to produce stress, it is vital that partners refrain from picking at the dissimilarities. As one Christian husband whose wife later converted told me: "Whenever possible, I did things the way she wanted them done. If she wanted to paint the bedroom blue, it was blue. If she wanted to go for an evening drive, we went."

If in your marriage you do not make every small difference a point of contention, you will be more apt to be taken seriously when something does arise that you feel merits discussion.

2. Speak with "I" messages, rather than "you" messages.

Communication experts agree that it is far less

threatening to express problems in terms of one's own feelings, rather than to accuse one's partner of causing the trouble. For example, it is much more effective to say something like "*I* feel lonely on weekends when you spend so much of your time with your church friends" than to say "*You* never stay home on weekends. You always have to be doing something for your church."

Speaking in "I" messages helps in the process of opening up your own feelings. And, according to Dolores Curran, author of *Stress and the Healthy Family*, communicating feelings is at the heart of a healthy marriage.[4]

3. Be aware of your own emotional investment in an issue and decide whether or not you are ready to deal with it at the current time.

Some issues are simply too hot to handle for a while. This is not to imply that there will never be a time when they might be confronted. However, only you know whether you can face up to certain issues right now. A number of factors might influence your decision to hold off on airing a grievance: a high level of other stress factors, a recent painful battle over the issue, an increasing strain on the relationship, or simply the knowledge that there is no point to acting on a given feeling.

There is a difference between *repressing* a feeling and *recognizing* a feeling and *deciding* not to act on it. There is nothing emotionally unhealthy about the latter.

4. Always, always show respect for your partner in any discussion you might have.

People do not have to agree, but there is a right and a wrong way to let another person know that your viewpoints may not be the same. Respect, says one author, is the "appreciation of the separateness of the other person."[5]

Lee F. Gruzen, in a sensitively done work entitled *Raising Your Jewish-Christian Child*, encourages interfaith couples to "work toward a fair marriage where mutual respect and self-respect can flourish." By "agreeing to disagree," she says, couples are "continually reminded how much they truly have in common." [6]

5. Attack the problems, not each other.

Often when a problem is aired, marriage partners react with a number of defensive patterns. As mentioned earlier, many of these are simply ways of preventing any type of definitive action on the part of one spouse or the other. If your spouse has brought up a particular issue that he or she feels is significant, take a look at what the concerns are. Look at the situation from every side you can. Avoid nonconstructive ways of dealing with the problem, such as lashing out at your spouse for the difference of opinion.

When I worked in public relations, we often developed new approaches by a process called brainstorming. Sitting around a table, my coworkers and I would suggest ideas. Each one would be written down—with nothing rejected or regarded as inferior. Later, in the evaluative stage, certain suggestions would be ruled out, with one emerging as the creative solution.

It would not be a bad idea for couples engaged in conflict over religious issues to do a bit of brainstorming. In this way the emphasis remains on solving the problem, not disparaging each other.

6. Stay on the subject.

It is easy to get caught up into an argument and to begin perpetuating it for its own sake, rather than to seek solutions to the initial grievance aired. If you are having conflict over how to spend your weekends, then by all means talk about such things as your love of the outdoors, or your spiritual commitment to be in church, or the importance of spending time together as a family. Don't let yourself get sidetracked into soliloquizing over your mate's family, who never go out together, or the time your spouse refused to attend the company picnic. Remember, the goal is to search for possible solutions. If a solution appears to be impossible, you will still have reached a measure of success if some headway has been made in the area of understanding each other better.

7. *Avoid generalities and extreme statements.*

Often when things have been building up for a long time, in the rush to express everything that has been waiting to be aired we go overboard. But by throwing a broad generality at our spouse, we only open up ourselves for retaliation.

When I taught freshman composition, I used to tell my college students not to use generalizations in their theme papers, since it would only take one exception to shoot down the entire thesis. The same can be said of an argument. If you hit your spouse with "You never attend church with the family," he or she can easily come back with "How can you say that? I was there on Christmas." The point quickly degenerates into a nitpicking game in which nothing constructive is accomplished.

8. *If you are really having trouble getting through a discussion that involves a lot of deep feelings on both sides, try rephrasing what your partner has said before speaking yourself.*

Although this method, suggested by David and Vera Mace in their Marriage Enrichment workshops, may at first appear to be a bit artificial, it insures that no one will make a comment before fully understanding what the other is trying to say. Don't assume that you have your partner all figured out—that because you have known him for 20 years, you can second-guess his motives, actions, and feelings before he even opens his mouth or makes one move. It might be surprising, as you rephrase his most recent comment, to find that your interpretation is not what he meant by his statement at all.

In an obvious state of despair and frustration, Cindy and Roger, married for just one year, arrived at our door. As they sat in the living room and attempted to apprise us of the growing problem in their home, they both carried on separate monologues chronicling the events of the past year from their own point of view. It was not until I asked them to stop and begin talking to each other, summarizing each previous comment before speaking themselves, that the two began to understand each other.

The oft-quoted verse "Help me seek not so much to be understood as to understand" is certainly pertinent here.

9. Don't feel that every discussion evolving out of conflict has to result in a mutual conclusion in order to be successful.

There are some subjects on which the two of you may never see eye-to-eye. However, there are other ways of coping with differences that can ease the stress. One expert advises using "trade-offs." [7] For example, if it is important to you that your spouse attend a Christmas pageant in which your daughter will play the part of an angel, agree to accompany him or her on a skiing trip the following week.

My own parents made an interesting trade-off with much greater ramifications. My father, a Protestant, agreed in the rectory on his wedding day to raise his children Roman Catholic. He reserved the right, however, to present his point of view to his children as they grew older. All four of us, along with my mother, later converted to his faith!

10. Once you have aired your thoughts, don't expect

your partner to change right away.

"I can't tell you how many times I've tried to tell Bob something, only to have him disagree vehemently," one young wife confided. "Yet I'm often surprised to hear him voicing my point of view to someone else a few days later."

Sometimes, simply having the opportunity to express how you feel has to be enough. You can never tell what the result might be in the long run. Marjorie, a new Christian and the breadwinner in her family, tried to express to her husband the importance of setting aside a certain percentage of her income for her church. But Tom just could not see it. Marjorie held off for a while, but her biblical explanation had not fallen on deaf ears. "Tom has grown to accept my tithing," she explains. "If ever we are short on money, he never throws it up in my face that I'm giving too much money to the church. He could, but he doesn't."

Conflict. It's not something to be generated for its own sake. As Paul states in Romans 12:18: "If it is possible, as far as it depends on you, live at peace with everyone" (NIV). Yet, as differences arise, it is impossible to avoid a confrontation while maintaining a healthy and open relationship. At such difficult times, the above principles become crucial to the survival of a marriage.

Notes

[1] Georgia Witkin-Lanoil, "Odd Couples," *Health*, September 1986, p. 77.

[2] *Sally Jessy Raphael*, May 1988.

[3] LaHaye, *How to Be Happy Though Married*, p. 99.

[4] Dolores Curran, *Stress and the Healthy Family* (New York: Harper and Row, 1985).

[5] Annie Gottlieb, "Respect: The Heart of Every Marriage," *McCall's*, April 1986.

[6] Lee F. Gruzen, *Raising Your Jewish-Christian Child* (New York: Dodd, Mead & Co., 1987), p. 41.

[7] Norman M. Lobsenz, "Do You Have a 'Green Thumb' for Marriage?" *Reader's Digest*, January 1987, p. 121.

Criticism:
A Destructive Force

3

I was looking for a misplaced book in the back seat of my car when I noticed her. She had parked at the far end of the lot. Her gaze seemed to be studiously avoiding the church and all it stood for.

But there she was, and I felt the need at least to establish contact. Hesitantly I knocked on her window. She rolled it down immediately, then turned to face me with cheeks wet from crying.

"Hello," I began, preparing to fish for my next words. But any reservations I had had about starting up a conversation proved needless.

"I'm here to pick up Richard," she began, "but I just can't face you people." She stopped for a moment, to see how her words were registering, then hurriedly went on. "Oh, I know you're good people, fine people— better than I'll ever be. I guess that's the problem."

"Would you like to go for a ride?" I asked. "They'll be busy inside for another 30 minutes or so."

As we drove down one country lane and up the next, her story tumbled out. Prayer meetings had become an excuse—an "unburdening time"—for Richard to relate all the difficulties of marriage to an unbeliever, she told me.

"I know what Richard talks about in there," Susan concluded. "And I feel that if ever I were to walk into that church, every head would turn in my direction, every neck would be craned to see who this horrendous person is whom Richard has put up with all these years. I've been branded—the non-Christian wife. If anything has kept me away from his church, that has."

As I listened to Susan's words, my heart went out to her—and to Richard. I could see him in prayer meeting every week, earnestly soliciting prayer for his wife while heads nodded sympathetically. I could hear his troubled sharing, fervent praying. How ironic that the very avenue through which Richard hoped to draw his wife into his church became the very means of closing her out!

The Christian spouse often has a real need—that of sharing struggles with fellow Christians. But when such sharing becomes the platform by which one spouse, in the name of religion, berates the other, then the sharing has become little more than glorified public criticism. This is a difficult issue for many people to face. The words are bitter, but they must be said: Even in the context of a prayer group, it is destructive to reduce marital tensions to black-and-white issues, with the non-Christian spouse as the culprit for *all* problems.

In his book *The Hurried Child,* David Elkind discusses the fact that the burden of stress in our society often causes us to view others as symbols, rather than complex human beings. His point is well taken and has serious implications for those involved in marriages in which one partner is viewed as "saved" and the other "unsaved."

He says, "People under stress tend to see other people in the shorthand of symbols, not the often hard-to-decipher longhand of personhood. Under stress, we see others as certain obvious, easily grasped stereotypes and abstractions. . . . Symbols, oversimplifications really, are energy-conserving. Parents under stress see their children as symbols because it is the least demanding way to deal with them. . . . Symbols thus free the parent from the energy-consuming task of knowing the child as a totality, a whole person." [1]

The question might well be raised: Are symbols freeing you of the energy required to know your spouse as a totality, a whole person? Has the issue of religion in the home led to oversimplification, stereotyping?

Elkind continues: "Symbols also conserve energy in another way. They are ready-at-hand targets for projecting unfulfilled needs, feelings, and emotions. Thus, by treating children as symbols, parents conserve the energy needed for coping with stress and have ready-made screens for projecting some of the consequences of stress, fear, anxiety, and frustration." [2]

Once again, we can apply his general principle to marriages in which religion has become a source of stress.

Has religion in your home become a "ready-at-hand target"? By treating your spouse as a symbol, are you conserving the energy needed for coping with stress, thereby creating a "ready-made screen" for projecting your feelings?

Such reduction of human beings to mere symbols can occur on the part of both spouses. As much as it can be destructive to view your spouse as "unsaved," it is equally destructive for your spouse to view you as a "religious fanatic." Human beings are more complex than that.

And as soon as we label another, Charles Cooley's "looking glass theory" comes into effect: People act out the part that they perceive others to be projecting on to them. In other words, the more your spouse feels that you view him or her in a particular stereotype, the more he or she will probably act out the part.

For the Christian, there is an even stronger reason to refrain from making a black-and-white, good-and-bad contrast between self and spouse. Says C. S. Lewis: "Whenever we find that our religious life is making us feel that we are good—above all, that we are better than someone else—I think we may be sure that we are being acted on, not by God, but by the devil." [3]

Pretty strong words to apply to the personal context of marriage! Yet although the thought is not a comfortable one, it bears some consideration. Do I, deep down, consider myself better than my spouse? And if so, how does this square with my understanding of the gospel?

The problem with categorizing is that no one has the ability to process all the things that have gone on in another's life and then to deduce where he should be at this particular point in time. We may feel that we know all there is to know about our spouse—her background and life experiences or his psychological makeup. But we can never stand in the place of God, judging someone else for the choices made.

The bottom line, as Eugene Durand has expressed it, is this: "Scolding is out; loving is in." [4] And loving can best be done in the context of respect and acceptance.

There is a branch of psychology called transactional analysis, which examines the levels on which individuals relate. We can play the part of a parent, a child, or an adult. Only by interacting with our spouses on an adult-to-adult level will respect be generated. If my spouse sees me in the role of a parent, like Jean (in the opening chapter of this book) who expresses strong disapproval of her husband's smoking, then he will react as a child, like Frank, who hides every time he feels the need to smoke.

The goal, then, is adult-to-adult communicating, free of criticism and censure. Quite a tall order at times, but the only way to insure growth and understanding in a marriage. Not only is criticism destructive to relationships and damaging to self-esteem, but as far as affecting a change is concerned, it simply doesn't work.

In preparing my master's thesis in the field of

communication, I ran across an interesting article[5] that discussed what happens when people feel their beliefs and practices are being attacked.

The researchers concluded that when people believe something strongly, they set up a sort of mental barrier, which goes into operation when they feel they are being attacked. Consequently, the harder you try to force a point, the more you criticize other people's beliefs, the more you are actually causing them to cling even more tightly to what they consider dear.

So why criticize? It brings dissension to marriage, destroys self-esteem, and doesn't work anyway! As Ed Wheat puts it, criticism never changes anyone for the better and "only puts miles of emotional distance between a husband and wife who may be secretly longing for closeness."[6]

Criticism can exist in a marriage on a number of levels. We have talked, primarily, about the deep dissatisfaction, the general sense of disapproval toward a mate's difference of lifestyle. But there is another type of criticism, which, if kept unchecked, can build to epidemic proportions. And that is the repeated, habitual picking at the little things.

I recall sitting in a Marriage Enrichment circle in which one woman was asked to comment on the statement "A nagging wife is like a dripping faucet." She was visibly uncomfortable for a few minutes, while her husband, beside her, looked pleasantly amused. Finally she responded, "Well, what do you do when someone won't listen? Some people don't leave you with much of a choice!"

It can be frustrating to live with a person who doesn't respond readily to your requests and promptings, but unfortunately, nagging and criticism only isolate an individual further.

Often the things about which people are most

critical appear rather trivial when voiced aloud. Think about it. What about your spouse causes you to bristle the most? Is it really worth your criticism?

An associate of mine becomes annoyed whenever her husband uses the expression, "In all honesty . . ."

"Why does he have to preface his remarks that way?" she asks. "Does he think I would assume he was not being honest if he hadn't clarified it?"

Like the proverbial fire in the book of James, criticism can start small and spread until it has engulfed an entire relationship. A strong-willed woman I met in one of our churches illustrates this point only too clearly.

Married for more than 30 years, Lillian and her husband experienced a parent-child relationship, in which Lillian played the role of the disapproving mother whose boy could do nothing right. The metaphor for her entire arsenal of criticism was the church. If only Tom would be converted. If he would join her church, everything would be all right. If he would stop all his bad habits, their marriage would be harmonious.

Then an ironic twist entered the picture. Tom did become interested in Christianity. After months of studying and soul searching, he decided to join her church. Shortly after, Lillian filed for divorce. Somehow she simply was not comfortable releasing the symbol she had held on to so tightly for so many years. She could not cope with an adult-to-adult relationship.

C. S. Lewis, in the opening of his book *Christian Behaviour*, begins with an illustration about a schoolboy who is asked to describe his picture of God. He replies that as far as he can make out, God is "the sort of person who is always snooping around to see if anyone is enjoying himself and then trying to stop it." [7] I wonder how many people today see their Christian spouses in that manner!

Trying to play conscience for someone else is like

trying to be an umpire in a baseball game in an adjoining field while you're up at bat in another. It simply can't be done with any success.

There is a colorful story of Aesop's that I always enjoyed as a little girl, and I think it would be appropriate to include it here. The tale is a familiar one and involves, as its three characters, the sun, the wind, and a man walking along the road. As this man makes his journey, the two elements of nature discuss the state of his cloak, which flaps loosely about his gaunt frame.

"I'll bet I can get that cloak off his shoulders," boasts the wind.

The sun, not to be outdone, responds, "I don't think so. But I'm sure I can."

Thus the contest begins. The wind sucks in all the forces of nature and lets forth a stream of breath, whipping the leaves from trees and stripping the loose grass from the hillside. But the man just clings more tightly to his cloak, determined not to lose it.

Next, it is the sun's turn. Smiling in all of his radiance, he comes forth with a full measure of warmth, concentrating his rays on the figure below. Immediately the man responds. With one spontaneous tug the cloak is off, and the man continues his journey down the road, his shoulders free of their heavy woolen burden.

Forcing an issue through coercion and criticism never works. But in an atmosphere of warmth and acceptance people are free to make the kinds of decisions that will best enable them to undertake their journey.

Notes

[1] David Elkind, *The Hurried Child* (New York: Addison Wesley, 1981), pp. 28, 29.

[2] *Ibid.*, p. 29.

[3] C. S. Lewis, *Christian Behaviour* (New York: MacMillan, 1944), p. 47.

[4] Eugene F. Durand, "How Not to Witness," *Adventist Review*, Nov. 3, 1988, p. 5.
[5] E. Katz, "On Reopening the Question of Selectivity in Exposure to Mass Communications."
[6] Ed Wheat, *Love Life for Every Married Couple* (Grand Rapids: Zondervan, 1980), p. 141.
[7] Lewis, p. 1.

Courtesy:
A Constructive Alternative

Kristy, a vivacious young woman with an infectious laugh, and Ted, her husband, attend church together every week with their three children. But it wasn't always that way.

"When I first met Kristy, I was trying to forget my religious upbringing," Ted told me as he sat on a folding chair in front of a camping tent. "Somehow I thought that if I tried hard enough, I could convince myself that spiritual things didn't matter."

But in the years that followed, Ted found himself sinking lower and lower into a depressive state. "It got to the point where I'd just wander into the back stairwell at work and sit there, smoking one cigarette after the other, wondering what life was all about. I was at a low ebb. A really low ebb."

Kristy, however, was not fooled by her husband's seeming apathy toward religion. "From the very beginning I could see something good in him. Somehow I could sense that he believed in God, that he faced an intense struggle deep within himself."

And that kind of sensitivity was just what Ted needed to help him break out of his downward cycle.

"Kristy's respect meant a lot to me through those tough times," Ted recalled. "I knew she believed in me, cared about me. And when things did begin to look up and I began to attend the church of my youth, she didn't try to corral me into her own church. She was just happy for me. Glad to know that some of my burden was easing."

Kristy's concern for Ted sprang not from an attempt to "witness" to him, not from a desire to do her "Christian duty," but from a heart full of genuine love for him, a respect for that within him which she identified as goodness.

All true courtesy within marriage springs from the same source: respect. Without it, a man and woman are simply two players following the rules while despising the game.

But what do you do when respect is gone, when that sense of esteem and real value you once held for your spouse has become eroded by time and words?

It might be interesting to start with the points about your spouse that annoy you the most, that call for the least courteous response on your part. It won't take long to come up with a mental list! Your mate's irritating traits of character are probably uppermost in your mind. After bringing to mind these "weak points," turn them over to their flip side—the corresponding positive traits that attracted you to your mate in the first place.

For example, Anne becomes annoyed when her husband constantly keeps her waiting, forgets to pass along phone messages, tosses magazines in a pile beside the bed. Yet a few moments of thought reveal that this is what attracted her to Larry in the first place—his easygoing nature, his ability to flow through time with a smoothness all his own, without being ruffled by details that would test most people to their limit.

Religion in the home often presents a similar set of positives and negatives. Cindy becomes exasperated by her Christian husband's attention to fine moral detail. When selling a car, he draws attention to all the flaws, lest he make a less-than-honest deal. When entering an amusement park with their just-turned-5 son, he is sure to purchase the 5-and-up ticket for his boy, pointing out the fact that although their son is small, he is, indeed, 5.

Yet in the midst of Cindy's exasperation, she has to admit that Larry's strength of conviction was one of his character traits that most appealed to her when she was searching for the man with whom she would spend the rest of her life. "I always felt like I wasn't strong enough spiritually," she says. "I wanted to find someone who could offer me the strength I didn't have, take up the cords of conviction where my own lines to heaven broke down."

And many strongly religious people, married to those whose concern over spiritual matters is minimal, have to admit, too, that part of the initial attraction was because of a certain carefree attitude, a lack of seriousness on the part of the other.

"My father was always very strict with me," says Sharon, a 30-year-old secretary married to the foreman of a small business. "When I was dating, I found myself wanting to be around someone who wouldn't monitor my every move, watching to see if I would slip up somehow."

Ten years later Sharon reminds herself of this as she attends church alone and holds up the religious standards of the home for her 4-year-old daughter. Her husband does not choose to involve himself with her religion, yet neither does he interfere with her right to practice it, or judge her conduct in relation to her own standards. That, feels Sharon, is something worth admiring.

True courtesy, then, is not some rigid adherence to formal rules of politeness, executed in much the same fashion as a high school student seeking to be elected

"Courtesy King," but a natural response, flowing out of a genuine respect for and recognition of the value of the other.

A film my husband and I have always enjoyed showing for Marriage Enrichment seminars is *Johnny Lingo.* The plot begins with a young man arriving on an island, intent on finding a wife among the inhabitants there. Much whispering and speculation ensues among the female population, because Johnny Lingo is an eligible bachelor in the finest sense of the word— handsome, wealthy, and, especially, wise. Most of the talk centers on which young woman Johnny Lingo will select and how many cows he will offer for her.

According to an old tribal custom, a prospective husband on the island secures a bride by offering her father a number of cows proportionate to the value of his daughter: the more attractive and winsome his daughter, the more cows a father could expect to receive.

Imagine the surprise of the entire village when Johnny Lingo selects Mahana, a downcast slip of a woman with little self-esteem and a face ravaged by despair. The talk continues, with many cruel comments and derisive laughter as once again the inhabitants of the town guess what the young man will offer for his bride. One cow? Two?

The married women on the island pick up the chatter as they boast over the price paid for their own hand in marriage. Some gloat over the fact that three cows were given; one or two even talk of five cows.

The day for the wedding finally arrives, and Johnny Lingo enters the village, driving his cows down the grassy path to Mahana's home. Townspeople step back in shock as they count the price put forth for this woman they hold in such low esteem. One, two, three . . . and the cows keep coming, bawling their way down the path, as if impatient to find their new home. Four, five, six . . . and yet another group of black-and-white beasts bellows its way around the corner. Seven, eight, nine, ten!

Ten cows! Never in the history of the village has such a high value been put on a woman! And Mahana! As the newly married couple skims across the bay in a bright, new canoe, the people of the village are left with much to talk about. In fact, the topic is still warm when, three months later, Johnny and Mahana return from their honeymoon.

And here is the climactic point of the movie. Tanned, laughing Johnny, rippling with muscles and good health, emerges from the vessel, and beside him is Mahana—poised, confident, and stunningly beautiful.

Once again the crowd is baffled. Once again there are questions, and a loud buzzing pronounces the interest of all. Later, when asked to explain his choice of a wife and his offer of such a high price, Johnny Lingo sums up the point of the movie in one cryptic statement. "I wanted it to be known all over this entire village that when Mahana was to be married, ten cows were given in exchange for her hand. Whenever the women gather in little groups and whisper over their washing, whenever the men toss remarks to one another across the wind, I want it to be known that Mahana is a ten-cow woman."

A simple parable. An obvious point. The more value you put on others and the more esteem you attach to their persons, the more those individuals will blossom forth with the natural grace and talent previously buried in the soils of their own disillusionment. That, in its essence, is true courtesy.

Says a Bible writer: "If anything is excellent or praiseworthy—think about such things" (Philippians 4:8, NIV).

Such counsel is at its richest when applied to the context of our own marriages and to the one with whom we have chosen to spend our lives.

There is much censure in the world in which we live. As the saying goes, it's a cruel, cold world out there, with irate motorists making stabbing accusations with each beep of the horn, insecure fellow workers seeking to cut with words and deception, apparent friends withdrawing support when their own needs are not met. The home is the one place where we can offer our mates a release from the tension, a "haven in a heartless world," as author C. Lasch puts it.[1]

I remember a small collection of photographs and quotations my sister sent to me when I moved to Michigan—a thousand miles from my New England home. Beside a picture of my family, involved in an animated discussion in the living room, she had penned in this statement of Frederick W. Robertson: "Home is the one place in all this world where hearts are sure of each other. It is the place of confidence. It is the place where we tear off that mask of guarded and suspicious coldness which the world forces us to wear in self-defense, and where we pour out the unreserved communications of full and confiding hearts. It is the spot where expressions of tenderness gush out without any sensation of awkwardness and without any sense of ridicule."

I have always treasured those words. As idealistic as they may sound, they represent a goal worth striving for. The place to start is with ourselves, our own willingness to tear off the mask of "guarded and suspicious coldness."

And whether we consider our spouse to be "too religious" or "far from salvation," the point remains. He or she is an individual worthy of our respect, our simple offering of human concern and kindness.

Steve, a 25-year-old non-Christian and separated from his wife for the past six months, relates the experience of living in a home in which courtesy is high on the list of vocabulary, but not a part of the reality.

"June is always so hung up with her religion," he says. "Calling this one, calling that one. I finally decided I couldn't take it any longer when one afternoon I lay on the couch, home from work, too sick to move. As soon as June came home she flounced right on by me, without even pausing to ask how I felt, and headed for the phone again, with all of her spiritual obligations and prayer lists."

Certainly we cannot read all that is happening in this marriage from this single statement of one partner's frustration. Yet we can get a renewed sense of the importance of courtesy—genuine warmth and concern—in a marriage.

In an article that appeared in the *Reader's Digest*, entitled "Ten Secrets Happy Couples Share," authors Connell Cowan and Melvyn Kinder list, as one of their ten points, the fact that "love is unselfish."

"While mature love requires a balance between giving and receiving, spontaneous unselfishness is the essence of love," they say. "Real love asks that we put our own needs on hold and respond to our mate's— not endlessly, not unilaterally, but often. In fact, we feel more 'in love' when giving to a partner than when receiving." [2]

Interesting advice, coming from authors of the popular book *Women Men Love/Women Men Leave*. One would almost expect it to be a quotation from a Christian handbook or a wedding sermon. But the principle is recognized in secular circles as well as Christian: Through giving we best express our love and strengthen our marriages.

And with such unselfishness comes not only the

desire to enfold our partner within the warmth of our love, but also the willingness to allow him or her the freedom to express his or her own individuality.

This can be a particular challenge in a marriage in which two partners hold different belief systems. It is so easy to fall into one of two extremes. On the one hand, I have seen couples who have no trouble allowing each other individuality—in fact, their entire relationship seems to be characterized by two separate lifestyles, with exchange of words being primarily for maintaining the "business" of the marriage. Jenny and Phil, one such couple, occupy the same home, yet have little else in common. Jenny attends her church functions, reads Christian books, and attempts to influence her children to follow her example. Phil surrounds himself with the "guys," fills his weekends with sports, and confines his contact with Jenny to such exchanges as "Have you paid the electric bill yet?" Clearly, neither seeks to control, yet unity is lacking.

On the other hand, I have watched the self-respect of individuals being washed away in the sea of control and dominance exerted by their partners. One young woman who attended a series of evangelistic meetings was thwarted on every side by her husband. When she finally did decide to become a member of a new denomination, he made his unhappiness perfectly clear. Each week as she pulls into her driveway after services, she prepares for the glowering face that will confront her as she steps into the house.

Sad to say, I have witnessed similar emotionally manipulative tactics on the part of a church-attending spouse. The innuendos, the digs, the strategically placed words—all intend to control, to reject the chosen lifestyle of another.

Real courtesy in marriage implies a respect of the individual, coupled with a concern for the other's welfare. It is a holding close, as well as a letting go; a relationship in which uniqueness and union are both held paramount.

The essence of the matter can probably best be summed up by Desiree, a young Christian wife, married to a man who does not choose to practice religion at this time. "I think the important thing, as far as religion in marriage is concerned, is talking about it and respecting the other person's point of view," she says. "God gave us a free will. We shouldn't try to take that away from each other."

Notes

[1] C. Lasch, *Haven in a Heartless World* (New York: Basic Books, 1977).

[2] Connell Cowan and Melvyn Kinder, "Ten Secrets Happy Couples Share," *Reader's Digest*, June 1988, pp. 201, 202.

Children:
The Most Difficult
Challenge

5

There is something about a child that brings us back to our own religious upbringing. Ideas and concepts that may have been buried for years come floating to the surface when a little face confronts us with "Who made the world?" or "Why did Grandma have to die?"

Children force us to take a stand—one way or another—on the issue of religion. And sometimes our renewed interest in spirituality is prompted before they are even born.

One mother of two preschool boys described her experience to me this way. "When my husband and I were dating, we rarely spoke about religion. Once we were married, however, and began to contemplate the arrival of children, the topic arose. Neither of us had attended church for quite some time. But I felt a sudden need to find something meaningful, . . . something more than the pseudoreligion my parents had demonstrated to me as a child when they dropped me off at Sunday school each week and then returned only to pick me up."

But Deborah discovered that once she had settled on a denomination that met her own needs, it was not so easy to persuade her husband to join her. Even more difficult was the fashioning of a philosophy of child-raising that incorporated her strong commitment to religion with her husband's lack of interest in spiritual matters.

"There are so many things that we are still trying to work through," she says. "How can I teach my child standards that are different from my husband's without conveying the message that Daddy is 'bad'? At what age are children equipped to make their own decisions concerning religious views? How can I encourage my children to go to church when Daddy is offering a day at the park to play football?"

But through the maze of questions, Deborah and Steve are finding some common areas, some positives to build on. "We both agree that there is a God, and that's a start," remarks Deborah. "And Steve agrees that our children should get some type of religious training. The specifics, however, are not so easy to work through."

Deborah is not alone. Her questions are asked again and again by those attempting to raise their children with a spiritual value system without putting down their spouse in the process. The deeper the commitment to religion, the more challenging and intense the problem becomes.

For some, the issues are not as difficult as those that Deborah and Steve face. "When I decided to take my daughter to church, my husband wasn't too crazy about the idea," a weekly church attender told me. "But once he realized that she was enjoying it, and I was not forcing her to go, he let off the pressure."

But the real challenge comes when a parent attempts not only to bring youngsters to church once a week, but also to establish a whole set of principles that will affect them every day of their lives. And while some feel that exposure to two different lifestyles can broaden a child's outlook and experience, others "see a potential for great confusion," according to Lawrence

Maloney in *U.S. News and World Report.*[1]

As a result, some parents in their frustration simply avoid the issue. "If Dennis sees it one way and I see it another, and we both believe our understanding to be from the Lord, how can we tell the children opposing things?" a mother of three cries out in frustration. "I've decided to stop having anything to do with teaching religion to the kids. They'll just have to get it in a parochial school."

But according to Dr. Ana-Maria Rizzuto, no child reaches school age without forming some image of God.[2]

So what's a parent to do? When value systems conflict, when a household threatens to appear hypocritical, and when the children become the focus of a power struggle with religion at its core, where do you turn for answers?

There are certainly no simple formulas for disentangling the myriad threads that constitute the conflicts which arise over rearing children in a "divided home." However, there are definitely some principles that can help provide understanding in the midst of the struggle.

1. First, and foremost of all, understand the stage of development that your children are in, and don't expect more than is reasonable from them in terms of religion.

Often, when two parents do not see eye-to-eye on religious matters, the children become the focus of disagreement, with both spouses anxiously pressing their views and lifestyle, in hopes of "winning out." This puts undue stress on the children, and expectations often arise that are not compatible with their emotional and intellectual development. James Fowler, in his classic book *Stages of Faith*, outlines the stages that an individual progresses through in understanding spiritual matters.[3]

It's encouraging to note that the first stage—that of young infants—is the time when the basics of trust, hope, and courage are established. And this forms the basis for all that comes later in faith development.

In other words, as you tend to the needs of your baby, you are ultimately setting the stage for his response to spiritual matters for the rest of the child's life. I find this to be especially good news for parents who are concerned about presenting religion to their children in homes with nonreligious spouses. Certainly you can give your baby lots of love and care without generating opposition on the part of your spouse. And this will constitute the basis for a lifetime of faith.

The next stage, which typically occurs during the preschool years, is characterized by children who naturally copy the adults they are close to. During this time, children can be strongly influenced by watching the parents—their moods, actions, visible faith.

Fantasy is also highly developed at this time, with children's imagination being unrestrained. During these years they are amassing a wealth of feelings and images that will surface in later years for evaluation and analysis. If anything is important during these years, it is the presence of a positive role model in children's lives. During these years children store up feelings and emotional responses that they will sort through later in life.

While children at this stage are not ready to handle the specifics of doctrine, they will respond readily to colorful stories and images. Their unrestrained imaginations make it easy for them to accept and visualize the characters of the Bible.

As children enter grade school, they begin the next phase of moral development. During these years, children are concerned with rules and fairness. "That's not fair," you hear them cry out time and again. Although their understanding of "the rules" may be far from balanced, they still are quick to point out what they see as "fair" or "not fair." During this stage it is important that children see portrayed clearly defined principles of behavior. When issues do not seem "fair" to them, they tend to reject the principles involved.

A second characteristic of this stage is children's deeply impressionable nature when it comes to story and drama. It is no surprise that dramatic presentations have such a powerful appeal to school-age children when one considers their general fascination with television. Because they are so vulnerable to narrative at this stage, it is important that children be given more than the standard fare of watered down ethics demonstrated on most TV programs, if a parent is concerned about spiritual training. Carefully selected Christian and nature videos, wholesome reading, creative church skits—all can have a positive impact on a child's development.

As your boys and girls leave their childhood behind and enter the turbulent years of adolescence, they begin to form their own value systems.

These are the delicate years, the time in which a parent must maintain a balance, giving direction, while offering the necessary freedoms. It is sometimes difficult for a dominant parent to face the fact that he or she is no longer the central figure in the child's life. While his or her role as counselor and model is in no way relinquished, the influence of significant others is very real, and the values of all will be sorted through and discarded or retained. When parents have differing value systems, these are difficult years for the children. As young people begin making observable choices, it is a challenge for a parent not to groan or cheer audibly as sides are taken. The best a parent can offer at this point is understanding, a listening ear, and compassion. Guidance is important, but as the child's teen years reach an end, parents must realize that ultimately the child is an individual who will make his or her own choices.

2. Accept the fact that your children are the product of two parents. Like it or not, your children will be exposed to the value system of your spouse.

Life would be so much easier if parents could predetermine all the input that would affect their offspring. But the complexity of human beings does not allow for such simplistic solutions to the challenge of child-raising. Nor would it be fair to impose the thinking of one individual upon another. In the final analysis, we must accept the blessings inherent in individuality and choices.

Thus it is crucial, in the quest to raise responsible, God-fearing children, to resist the urge to shelter them from all thinking that differs from your own, particularly that of your spouse. Such an attempt is not only futile; it also conveys the message that you are insecure over your own beliefs.

Lee F. Gruzen, author of *Raising Your Jewish-Christian Child*, quotes child psychiatrist Morton Hodas as saying: "When they're asked to identify themselves, children will always establish a connection to both parents. Who you are is a very concrete thing to a child. He'll always tell you, 'I came from her, I came from him.' " [4]

3. Find something of mutuality, no matter how small, to build on.

Like Deborah and Steve, who find strength in the fact that both believe in God, couples can garner courage in knowing that there are some elements in their philosophy of religion and child-raising which are shared. Such acknowledgment helps to bond husband and wife together, and offers the child at least a small sense of spiritual unity.

It may be difficult at first to discover anything at all that you have in common with your spouse in the area of spirituality. But there are certain givens of fairness and right that are natural assumptions of human living. In his book *Mere Christianity* C. S. Lewis discusses the fact that a person standing in line will be instantly offended if another strides to the head with no recognition of the necessity of waiting his or her turn. Such an ingrained sense of justice, says Lewis, is an evidence of the powers of right and wrong in the universe.[5] If you can find nothing else to build on, surely your spouse becomes offended if someone cuts in front of him or her in line! Thus the value of justice can be transmitted to your children.

4. Accept the fact that there are some issues of child-raising that you and your spouse will never resolve.

Talking is important in a marriage, and the more communication, the stronger the relationship. But there comes a point where the better part of wisdom is to let the issue lie, at least for a while.

"We are continually discussing our beliefs, and how they affect our relationship," a bride of six months told me. "We plan on having children, but there are some things about raising them that we will probably never agree on. When neither of us can see a solution and we sense the frustration beginning to mount, we just stop talking for a while."

5. Be aware that you are modeling the effects of the message you preach. If your children view you as secure and happy, they will ultimately deduce that your value system has offered meaning and significance to your own life.

Often parents who are anxious to teach their children to read at a young age expose them to everything from flash cards to workbooks, only to discover later that their children spend little or no time in recreational reading. The bottom line in getting children to read, the authorities tell us, is modeling the reading habit ourselves. If your children frequently see you deriving pleasure from a book, they will want to do the same.

The same is true of transmitting a value system. If your children view your life as a constant drudgery, beset by do's and don'ts, it will be difficult for them to want to emulate you. If, on the other hand, they see your outlook enabling you to enjoy life and gain courage to deal with its difficulties, they will desire the same for themselves.

6. Remember that the ultimate goal of child-raising is self-control and self-discipline.

Says James Dobson, popular author and speaker on family topics: "Parents should introduce their child to discipline and self-control by the use of external influences when he is young. By being required to behave responsibly, he gains valuable experience in controlling his own impulses and resources. Then as he grows into the teen years, the transfer of responsibility is made year by year from the shoulders of the parent directly to the child. He is no longer forced to do what he has learned during earlier years." [6]

And the sooner children can take responsibility for their own actions, the stronger their self-concept will become and the more they will learn to act from principle. A Christian mother of a 7-year-old girl and 8-year-old boy, married to a man who displays little interest in family values, relates this story:

"From the time the children were very little, I have had to remove them from the room when Daddy brings home R-rated movies and shows no concern over what the children are being exposed to. And apparently some message has gotten across to Justin and Jennifer. Just yesterday I returned from a shopping trip to be told by the kids, 'Daddy was watching some stuff that wasn't too good, so we played Parcheesi® in the dining room.' I was so pleased to know that they had made such a decision for themselves."

7. When children enter young adulthood and have decided on a value system, accept them unconditionally.

An individual will never be won to anyone's faith or encouraged into a more positive lifestyle by feeling shame or alienation. The reality of having raised a child who has decided to reject your values is painful and often produces feelings of guilt. The tendency can be to take it out on a son or daughter, communicating disfavor in every possible opening in conversations. But such an attitude only puts more distance between ourselves and our children, removing any possibility for restoration.

Stacey, a 30-year-old woman who does not attend church, enjoys the support, concern, and love of her conservative Protestant family. Laura, who rejected family values, is held in contempt by her 'religious' mother and loved only conditionally: "If you forsake your ways, you'll be accepted back into the circle of my love." Which person, would you guess, is in a more vulnerable position to respond ultimately to family values? And in the event that neither Laura nor Stacey ever returns to the standards of her youth, which family has lost everything?

Notes

[1] Lawrence D. Maloney, "Behind the Rise in Mixed Marriages," *U.S. News and World Report*, Feb. 10, 1986, p. 71.

[2] Ana-Maria Rizzuto, *The Birth of the Living God* (Chicago: University of Chicago Press, 1979).

[3] The stages discussed are presented in detail in James Fowler, *Stages of Faith* (San Francisco: Harper and Row, 1981).

[4] Gruzen, *Raising Your Jewish-Christian Child,* p. 46.

[5] C. S. Lewis, *Mere Christianity* (New York: MacMillan, 1952), p. 17.

[6] Dr. James Dobson, *The Strong-willed Child* (Wheaton, Ill.: Tyndale House, 1978), p. 66.

Coping:
Weekends, Holidays,
and In-laws

6

The weekend. Life's answer to a hectic week of working, shopping, and shuttling. A time for relaxation, entertainment, family togetherness. "Thank goodness it's Friday." Forty-eight hours of sheer enjoyment. Or is it?

To numerous couples whose religious interests differ, the motto has been changed to "Thank goodness it's Monday."

As I sat in on a support group for Christian women with non-Christian husbands, I was deeply moved by the intensity of their emotions and the honesty with which they shared them.

"I dread weekends," began one woman with three children. "My husband grabs a beer can and just plants himself in front of the television, while I try to keep the kids under control. I really believe the house could fall down around him and he wouldn't even know it. He'd just sit there, his eyes glued to the TV, while the rest of us scrambled to get out."

"And then there's the church scene," she said and glanced furtively in my direction, suddenly feeling her vulnerability with a "foreigner" in the group. "Every week it's the same thing. I get the kids all dressed, and Daddy suddenly comes up with something exciting to do. It's like his ego can't handle the fact that I'm doing something to influence them toward my way of thinking."

Others chimed in, and the discussion continued unchecked for the next hour. Some aired problems; others offered advice. Said one woman whose two boys are often invited on special trips by Dad just as they prepare to leave for church: "I've found that it's just not worth the hassle of fighting it out every week. I used to make a big issue out of taking the boys with me. But I've learned to give in a little. If Ken wants to take them fishing, I let him take them fishing. Invariably he lets up on the pressure after that, and I have no trouble taking them with me to church the following week."

The conversation swung from Saturdays and Sundays to special occasions, and I discovered that if weekends are not exactly the pot of gold at the end of a weekly rainbow, holidays are even more disillusioning. Differences of beliefs, values, and outlook become magnified, with tempers flaring or families on edge tiptoeing around the house. One woman, whose emotional words triggered the idea for the title of this book, discussed the "holiday problem" at length. "I've always felt that the focus at holiday time should be on the spiritual aspect of things," she said. "But I really have to downplay that in my family. Just to get a blessing said at the Thanksgiving table is a major feat."

While driving home after the meeting, I replayed much of the conversation in my mind. I realized that these women, all part of a 1,000 member Congregational church, were not just nominal Christians, but strongly committed believers. The strength of their commitments made working out a plan with their nonbelieving husbands more difficult than some others I had spoken with. Their principles were simply too important to compromise. They bent when they could, but there was much inner wrestling over the issues.

I couldn't help thinking of one woman I had inter-viewed earlier who had made things sound so easy. "I'm a Protestant, but I don't have a strong identity with one particular faith," she told me. "Each year I present both Christian and Jewish traditions to my children during the holiday season. My husband, whose Jewish upbringing was quite secular, doesn't have a problem with a Christmas tree, and I'm very comfortable with Hanukkah lights."

It would be nice if all problems between spouses with differing beliefs were solved so easily at holiday time. But unfortunately, such is not the case.

What can be done on weekends and holidays, when the family is suddenly in the spotlight and the harsh glare only serves to illuminate differences?

I like these words of Michael Grant, quoted in San Diego's *Union:* "We will always be different. I think of anniversaries as a time for roses and dinner; she prefers Mexican food and a movie. For Halloween she thinks apples are a good treat. I say Since when did Halloween have anything to do with nutrition?

"Don't mistake it for a solid marriage. There is no such thing. Marriage is more like an airplane than a rock. You have to commit the thing to flight, and then it creaks and groans, and keeping it airborne depends entirely on attitude. Working at it, though, we can fly forever. Only she and I will know how hard it has been, or how worthwhile."

Perhaps you don't feel as though your airplane is even moving down the runway, let alone enabling you to "fly forever," but Michael Grant has hit upon a key concept here: the importance of attitude in making a relationship work.

And this is the very topic that the support group eventually focused in on. One woman, married to an alcoholic, shared these thoughts: "I'm learning more and more that everything has to do with attitude. It used to be that I would not drink — and feel pious about it. Every time my husband asked me why I chose to refrain, I would get on my little soapbox. My attitude conveyed my message clearly — 'You're a loser and I'm not.'

"But I've changed my attitude now; I'm not so self-righteous," she continued. "When he asks me why I don't drink, I merely tell him it doesn't taste good to me anymore. And he no longer becomes angry about it. In fact, we are even finding that we can laugh over our difference."

As I listened, I was impressed that although this woman's life was not easy and her husband had a tendency toward verbal abuse, she was committed to making their relationship work, to keeping their vessel airborne, amid the creaks and groans.

The importance of attitude cannot be overestimated when it comes to weekends. Every weekend is the basis for the next; every thought and feeling beds down for a week and rises again at the end of seven days. If you face the weekend like a migraine coming on, it will surely be the throbbing headache you anticipate. And the downward cycle will be repeated, and repeated, and repeated.

But before you give up in despair, consider breaking out of the cycle. There are two parts of the weekend that married couples with religious differences must face: the free time, which suddenly throws the whole family together under one roof, and the clash of secular desires and spiritual interests between spouses.

It is vitally important that spouses plan some activity together on a regular basis over the weekend. It might seem impossible to find something that both are interested in, but don't give up. Perhaps a wife loves to go out and do things, and a husband would prefer to stay home every weekend. Or maybe a husband is activity-oriented, and would opt for swimming, bowling, and skiing, whereas the wife craves an electric blanket and a good book.

Whatever the case, find something you can do together, which both of you can look forward to. Perhaps something as simple as going out to eat together each Saturday night. Can't afford it? Concerned that the drinking issue will cause even more problems? Go out for breakfast. Many places hang out a shingle offering a morning meal for as little as 99 cents, and it is unlikely your spouse will make an issue of drinking early in the morning. Worried about the kids? Ask a neighbor to help you out for an hour, or pay a teenager to watch the children while you're gone. You're worth it.

Just make a commitment, and follow through on it. A little creative effort and planning can result in a reversal of the mind-set that causes you to dread weekends before the week is even half over. And such an effort might reap rewards in your marriage even after the weekend is over.

I think of a middle-aged couple who lived in my neighborhood when I was a child growing up. Madeline, a devout Catholic, and her husband of 20 years, Roy, faced a deteriorating relationship, which was all too evident to those of us who inhabited homes around them. On weekends Madeline sat home while Roy frequented the bars in the center of town. Long after Madeline turned in for the night, Roy arrived home— weaving and incoherent. Through some stroke of luck the pair decided to try their hand at tennis one weekend, and came home exhausted but happy. Lessons followed, and the two developed a whole new identity centered on the sport. They now had something in common, something to look forward to rather than dread at week's end. Roy slacked off on his drinking; Madeline found herself with a new and enjoyable companion.

It is surprising what spending a little special time with a spouse each weekend can do for a marriage.

"I'm just now realizing that I've always put my kids before my husband," says Maggie, an evangelical Christian. "And the conviction is settling on me that my order is all wrong."

But what about the other part of the weekend, the part that you cannot share at this point in your life—"the church scene," as it has been described? As a religious spouse, how can you manage a graceful exit, minimize the conflict over the children, dedicate the day to God? As a spouse with no interest in religious matters, how can you retain your own identity, feel comfortable in your own home, have time with your own kids?

The answers do not come easily, and they must be worked out within the context of each home. "At first Sabbaths were a difficult time for me," says a convert to the Seventh-day Adventist faith. "My husband did not understand my faith, and he would ask me to do things that I did not feel comfortable with. But now, after a year, he has come to understand what I will and will not do."

It's important to work out an understanding, be it tacit or verbal, of exactly what is going to happen each week regarding the church scene. If one spouse is not comfortable attending church, it's not fair to put on the pressure or slip in the barbed guilt trips each week. If the other considers religion important, it should be clear just what the commitments involve and how they will impact on the family's interaction in the course of the weekend.

It may not be easy to state your beliefs and the

implications of them clearly and without hesitation, but after the initial confrontation you will find it much easier to follow through on your convictions once your spouse knows exactly what to expect.

As for the children, it is much wiser to bring up the subject the evening before the church scene and to get things out in the open before they erupt. Find out if your spouse has plans for the kids. Express your concerns. Decide how both of you can have time with the children without compromising their religious training. It should be noted here that psychologists do recommend that if one spouse is concerned about religion and the other is not, the religious spouse should be the one responsible for the spiritual training of the children. In this way, the children are at least exposed to something, and are free to accept or reject it when they reach the age of accountability.

This may be easier said than done in your home, but the important thing is to keep the avenues of communication open. It might seem much easier to sneak out in the morning with the kids before a spouse even wakes up, but each time an opportunity for communication is missed, one more brick is added to the wall of separation and isolation between a religious and non-religious spouse. If you are not communicating, start somewhere, somehow. Even a tiny step is better than no progress at all. And it is something to build on.

Like weekends, holidays are occasions that should be brought out in the open in advance to minimize spontaneous conflicts over differences in religion. Holidays can be even more difficult, since they involve not only the immediate family, but relatives as well. A neighbor told me candidly, "My in-laws are even less tolerant of my religious beliefs than my husband is. And when they're around, I feel that any support I might have gotten from my husband has vanished."

And when grandchildren enter the picture, things become even more complicated. "My parents disowned us when we joined the church. They became so angry that they wouldn't even speak to the children for years," a member of a large Protestant denomination expressed to me during an interview. "Even now my mother makes an issue of taking my kids to her church and teaching them all her prayers."

And such a situation is not uncommon. In an article that appeared in the August 1988 issue of *Parenting* magazine, the authors make this comment: "Any problems involving your spouse's parents are only magnified when children enter the picture and the in-laws become grandparents—which is a bit like attorneys becoming judges. Opinion becomes law, and any deviation from the prescribed path is met with [contempt]." [1]

How do couples handle such interference? The article goes on: "Parents employ many tactics in dealing with the unwanted advice of their mate's makers. Some follow it to the letter, while others choose to ignore it. Other parents simply refuse to allow the spouse's folks to rule; the chain of command begins with the parents, and no Alexander Haig of an in-law is going to change that." [2]

The bottom line is that the ultimate choice in raising your children belongs to you and *not* to your parents or in-laws. But since your children will be exposed to a number of relatives at holiday time—even those who might be manipulative or difficult—it is important to teach them a basic respect and understanding of the rights of others to their own beliefs.

In the final analysis, it is the relationship between yourself and your spouse and how you will sift the advice, commands, and injunctions of parents and in-laws through the mesh of your marriage that is important.

George Target, in *These Times* magazine, authored a beautiful piece entitled "A Love Stronger Than Hate." In it he related the story of Ian, a man of "good Protestant stock, the sort that goes to church twice every Sunday as regular as the proverbial clockwork." Walking home from work one afternoon in Northern Ireland, Ian was hit by a terrorist's bomb and afflicted with sudden blindness. And who should nurse him, during his four months in the hospital, but Bridget, a woman of "good Catholic stock, the sort that goes to Mass first thing every Sunday morning."

You can guess the conflict that arose when Ian and Bridget announced plans for marriage. "Their families were appalled. Thinking of getting married? The very law of God forbade it, surely."

And so the two were driven apart, until the most climactic part of the story. Bridget, trapped in a bombed building, is rescued by the blind Ian, who is the only one who can find his way to her in the darkness of the collapse. And once again the two take up "their love from where they had never really left it."

The ending of the story offers hope for all whose parents oppose their marriage, for all whose in-laws cast aspersions upon their beliefs, for all who live in a divided home.

"True, both families resisted every step of the way. And there was one dramatic confrontation between them that almost led to a fistfight: shouted abuse, insults, desperate threats. But in the middle of it Bridget took Ian's hand. . . . And [together] they walked out of that place of hatred.

"Yes, they would marry. Yes, all the conventional wisdom warns of failure. But do you know a more excellent way than love? . . . And what other healing is there?"[3]

Notes

[1] "The Long Arms of the In-laws," *Parenting*, August 1988, p. 64.
[2] *Ibid.*, p. 64.
[3] George Target, "A Love Stronger Than Hate," *These Times*, January 1984, pp. 3, 4.

Commitment: Making It Work

7

In his popular book entitled *Caring and Commitment: Learning to Live the Love We Promise*, Lewis B. Smedes devotes 176 pages to the topic of commitment in marriage. Included in his book is the idea that commitment is for keeps, a notion often regarded lightly in the self-actualization era in which we live. I like what Professor Smedes says concerning commitment and change.

"I won't be quite the same person tomorrow that I am today. I will change. My needs will change. My desires will change. So will my feelings.

"When I promise to be with you, I do not know for sure what I will be like at some distant time when you will need me. Yet I expect that the person I will become will keep the commitment that I make today.

"You will change as much as I will. I do not know what you will be like in some distant tomorrow. Will you be attractive? Healthy? Will you change your mind about the important things we both believe in now? Will you feel differently about me? Will you want me to be near you? How can I know for sure?

"Yet I expect to keep my commitment to you, whoever you turn out to be in the future. . . .

"A commitment has a 'no matter what' quality about it. No matter how I change. No matter what happens to you. No matter what happens around us. It has the feel of *unconditionality*.

"What a risk!

"And how high the stakes!" [1]

What Smedes is describing here is no mild promise, no fleeting feeling of love. And to some the implications are more far-reaching than to others. Perhaps there has been a drastic change in you or your spouse or your circumstances since the day when stars played before your eyes as you uttered "I do."

I think of the many couples whose paths have crossed mine through the years. The idealistic young woman who married a doctor-in-training, yet broke her commitment to him when he dropped out of medical school two years later to pursue a career in photography.

And on the other side of the spectrum, my own father-in-law, who married an attractive, talented nurse—only to discover 20 years later that she was becoming the victim of Parkinson's disease, a totally debilitating illness that prevented her from even bringing a spoon to her mouth. True to his commitment, he cared for her faithfully until the day he died.

The only thing that stays the same, it has been aptly stated, is that things change. At such times, commitment is put to its ultimate test. Often in a marriage change comes about in the realm of religion. Having served with my husband in five different congregations, I've had many an opportunity to struggle through the stress of change with couples, rejoicing with some at victories, mourning with others over the loss of a relationship. I think of Kara, who married an all-American physical education teacher whose every minute centered on basketball, swimming, and track. Three years after their marriage he found himself sitting in an auditorium and being awed by a preacher presenting principles that were totally new to him. The radical change of lifestyle that followed was too much for Kara. Breaking her commitment, she ended the relationship.

I hurt, still, when I remember Tamara. Burned once in a marriage by a cruel, manipulative man, she determined never again to marry until she had found someone who shared her deep commitment to religion. How blessed she felt when she discovered Harris. The two dated for a year, attending church together, seemingly sharing a similar Christian perspective. Shortly after their marriage, however, he backed out of the spiritual field entirely and became angry whenever Tamara mentioned religion. Within a year the two were separated.

Change in marriage. Think about it. Have you undergone a change in your own life in the area of religion? Put yourself in your spouse's shoes for a moment. What must it be like to feel that you know a person, only to be confronted with a whole new value system, a whole new person, in essence? The hanging on despite the change is what commitment is all about. But it is not always easy.

Or perhaps your spouse has changed—gone from a caring, warm person you once felt very loving toward to a withdrawn, mysterious element in the background; from tolerant to angry; from social drinker to alcoholic. What then?

This is when commitment becomes not just a word, but a way of life. "I don't feel any love toward my husband anymore," a 30-year-old Christian wife admitted to me. "And I want the feeling. I'm a feeling person. But right now I'm learning just to trust in the Lord day by day. It's hard to do, but I know the feelings will come according to His time clock."

Ed Wheat, in his book *Love Life*, spends one chapter describing "agapé love"—the New Testament love that is "unconditional, unchanging, inexhaustible, generous beyond measure, and most wonderfully kind." [2] This chapter has been the hope of many people wedded to those who offer little or nothing to the relationship. "I cling to that chapter," the above woman confided to me recently. "Whenever I become discouraged or things get really bad, I read it over and over."

Dr. Wheat suggests that we begin by evaluating our own approach to love to determine whether we presently love conditionally or unconditionally. He lists a series of questions that get at the heart of the matter by analyzing our true motives. Is our love based on behavior and performance—or is it constant despite change and undesirable traits in our partner?

He then goes on to encourage his readers to shower their partners with true agapé love—the love of principle that rides high above the pettiness of everyday annoyances.

Clearly, agapé love requires a total commitment of one's whole self if it is to be genuine. There will be days when you want to give up in despair. "I'm tired of being the one who always tries," says one wife who manages to hold down a full-time job, take responsibility for the children, and keep her marriage together by a slim thread. "I want my marriage to work. But it gets old fast—this constant giving, and sharing, and trying—all by yourself."

It is a challenge, but agapé love, with its giving nature, has its rewards, too. For it is through giving that we forget ourselves and sense our highest joy.

Yet it sometimes seems that this generous giving, this unconditional loving, this devotion unrelated to performance, goes against our very nature. From the time we are very small, we learn that life is made up of pleasing and disappointing, reward and punishment, merits and demerits. We come to associate performance with a grade, good behavior with a bountiful

Christmas, obedience with acceptance.

Such oversimplification may help make our childhood a bit easier, but it will never do in establishing the significant relationships so important to our life. Love offered only under certain conditions is really not love at all, but subtle manipulation.

Unconditional love is crucial, because it is actually the deepest longing of the human heart. We all need to be loved, not because we are physically attractive, or keep a clean house, or bring home a healthy paycheck, but simply because we are who we are. When we are loved for some external reason, there is always that element of doubt, insecurity—if I don't continue to measure up, the affections will be cut off. How many people reach adulthood with a fragmented self-concept because they are still trying to earn that love which was never real to begin with!

Agapé love, that deep caring and devotion not because of but in spite of, is the greenhouse that provides just the right environment for strength and growth. By loving unconditionally, we surround our spouse with a shelter of warmth and light that will fortify him or her for all of the struggles in life.

This basic need for agapé love, for that affection showered regardless of performance, has been described aptly by an eighth-grade student whose theme I graded for an English competency exam administered by the state of Connecticut. "Pretend that you would like to become a member of a club," the student was asked. "Describe the club, then discuss your qualifications and why you believe the club ought to select you." Bypassing the usual selections of student government, sports, and music clubs, the student wrote: "I would like to become a member of a society that had no entrance requirements. The only rules in this society would be that each person would be accepted, no matter what. It would not matter if a person had poor grades, or was not good at sports, or didn't get along with the faculty or his parents. Each person would be respected and accepted, just like everyone else."

Here is a person crying out to be accepted! I am reminded of a character in Katherine Anne Porter's *Ship of Fools*, who cries out in desperation: "Love me. Love me in spite of all! Whether or not I love you, whether I am fit to love, whether you are able to love, even if there is no such thing as love, love me!" [3]

Commitment in marriage means just that. Loving someone in spite of all. Loving someone whether or not he or she is fit to be loved. Loving out of principle, when the feelings are not there. Loving unconditionally, "no matter how I change, no matter what happens to you, no matter what happens around us."

Commitment in a marriage between individuals with differing religious perspectives means even more. It means loving you whether or not you agree with me, whether or not you support my value system, whether or not you pray to my God. It means seeing you as an individual worthy of respect, accepting you for who you are, giving of myself with no ulterior motive for change on your part. And while I am loving you unconditionally, I owe it to our relationship to do the same for myself. Commitment means not only accepting my spouse, but believing in myself also, affirming my own personhood. I like the words of Cecil Osborne, author of *The Art of Learning to Love Yourself.* "Those with a positive regard for themselves tend to flow with life, instead of fighting it. They feel more in harmony with the universe, less out of synchronization. Life becomes less of a struggling, crushing, competitive game where someone always loses and some may get hurt." [4]

Thus it does not take away from my spouse for me to regard myself favorably, but rather adds to the quality of our relationship. Once I accept myself, I am in a better position to accept others. Dr. Maurice Wagner in his book *The Sensation of Being Somebody* says that attempting to reach out to others while focusing on our own feelings of inadequacy can be compared to trying to spit and swallow at the same time![5] It simply can't be done. I must be comfortable with who I am before I can love you unconditionally.

It takes a lot of courage at times to take the steps needed to fortify our own emotional reserves. But it is important not only for ourselves, but for all those whose lives we touch, particularly if we find ourselves linked to those whose own self-esteem is damaged. I came across an article in the newspaper recently with a title that piqued my interest—"Here's Help for Those Married to Weird Spouses." [6] In it Philadelphia psychiatrist Alan Summers discusses four different character types—people who manage to make life miserable for themselves and those around them.

First is the "parsimonious" individual, who "not only guards his money but . . . also sits tightly on his emotions, and getting him to utter a gracious, approving word is a major task." If you are married to such an individual, says Summers, it is crucial for you to get support from somewhere to make up for what is lacking at home. He suggests support groups and outside activities as possible avenues for dealing with the feelings of emptiness and deprivation. Once you begin to feel affirmed, you will be better able to function in the home.

If you are married to a "conforming" individual who "stands for nothing," says Summers, your life is made up of an experience similar to "trying to push off against a wall made of gelatin." He suggests making gradual changes in your own life and slowly introducing your spouse to the new things you're doing.

The last two types of individuals—the "inflexible" and the "arrogant"—are those who make life difficult not by being passive, but by active opposition. The inflexible individual is one who can't deal with change and thus falls apart and becomes irrational whenever things appear to be different. The arrogant person is "self-righteous, authoritarian, vindictive." He communicates the fact that he is always right and warns those who argue with him, "Don't cross me."

The strategies for dealing with these two types of spouses are actually very different, according to Summers. If your spouse appears to be inflexible, it is best to assert yourself and make it clear that you will not be dominated by his or her fear of change. "Maybe you'll take separate vacations, visit relatives by yourself," says Summers. "When the inflexible person complains, discuss the changes you desire. Get a dialogue going." In the case of religious differences, it is important to clearly establish your own identity.

If you are married to an arrogant person, however, a lighter approach is necessary, according to Summers. Here is where true agapé love comes into focus. With an arrogant person, "your feelings of outrage may be similar to when you're in a relationship with somebody who's inflexible, but you can't use the same strategy. Your self-esteem is too low to try it, and an arrogant person will respond negatively to it. His pride always is at stake, and anything heavy-handed is likely to backfire. Work on yourself. Get professional help for your damaged pride. Then lavish praise and admiration on your spouse and avoid getting into power struggles. If it's hard for you to do, say that you're trying it just for a year. Let him have his way as much as possible."

Thus commitment in marriage means accepting your spouse, loving him or her with all of his or her idiosyncrasies, putting no conditions on your affections. But while you are doing this, it is important to realize your own need for support and affirmation. A well that is dry cannot pour forth water, no matter how intense the need. By being honest with yourself and accepting the fact that your marriage will be benefited as your own esteem is heightened, you will ultimately live out the highest form of commitment.

Notes

[1] Lewis B. Smedes, *Caring and Commitment: Learning to Live the Love We Promise* (San Francisco: Harper and Row, 1988), p. 9.

[2] Wheat, *Love Life for Every Married Couple*, p. 119.

[3] Quoted in: Douglas Cooper, *Living God's Love* (Mountain View, Calif.: Pacific Press, 1975), p. 39.

[4] Cecil Osborne, *The Art of Learning to Love Yourself* (Grand Rapids: Zondervan, 1976), p. 96.

[5] Maurice Wagner, *The Sensation of Being Somebody* (Grand Rapids: Zondervan, 1975).

[6] Darrell Sifford, "Here's Help for Those Married to Weird Spouses," Bridgeport, Connecticut, *Post*.

Crisis:
The Making or Breaking
of a Relationship

------------------- 8 -------------------

A nd now I have told you before it takes place, so that when it does take place, you may believe" (John 14:29, RSV).

This statement, made by Christ in reference to His death and resurrection, illustrates the fact that there are times when knowledge gained in advance is crucial to survival. Such is true in the case of a crisis.

Certainly people do not wish a crisis upon themselves or their families. But it is important to understand just what can and does happen to relationships embroiled in traumatic events, particularly when couples do not begin by sharing the same outlook.

The main factor, in the event of a crisis, is that people suddenly become very vulnerable to change — which can have some very positive or negative effects on their lives and relationships. Howard Clinebell, whose text is a standard for courses in pastoral counseling, says: "A crisis is more than simply a time of pain and stress to be endured. . . . It is a turning point toward or away from greater personality wholeness." [1]

Lee Gruzen, in her work concerning Jewish-Christian marriages, cites an example of a traumatic event being the catalyst for returning to religion. "Sometimes a crisis is necessary to force a choice and a reevaluation," she says, referring to a New York City artist whose younger brother was suddenly killed in a boating accident. "In the face of that traumatic loss, the woman found herself relying upon her religious beliefs and her Protestant family for comfort and assurance. The factors that had dampened her religious commitment for years before the accident—her Jewish husband's lack of religious conviction and, in her eyes, the disappointing models her parents had become—no longer mattered or dictated her plans for her children." [2]

Yet such a return to religiosity in the face of adversity is not always the case. I will never forget the day my husband preached on the love of God and was met at the door by an angry, crying woman whom he had never met before. "My oldest son was killed in a car accident," she said. "You will never know what it means to discover that your God is not so loving as you once believed."

And as much as a crisis can radically affect the thinking of one person, it can strongly affect the relationship between individuals as well. Joy Swift, in her first-person account *"They're All Dead, Aren't They?"* relates the tragic story of the loss of five children: one to terminal illness, and four to the bullets of a teenage murderer. In the aftermath of such an overwhelming crisis, Joy and her husband turned to religion for comfort. But when Joy's interest in the Bible deepened, a rift began to develop in the relationship.

"George and I had always agreed on everything—or at least we could each bend a little to see the other's point of view. We had always shared the same goals and dreams and priorities. Why couldn't we share our faith in God? Why did it have to hurt so much to stand for what I believed was right?

"I never thought anything would come between us. I certainly never thought it would be the Bible!" [3]

Fortunately, Joy and George were able to work

things through, as George grew to understand that Joy's convictions would not be compromised. However, not all marriages fare as well in the event of a tragedy. Along with the pain and loss often come anger and blame toward one's spouse, resulting in walls of separation. And as individuals deal with tragedy in their own way, they sometimes find their lives taking on new directions, away from those they love.

What can you do, in the event of a crisis, to minimize the strain between yourself and your spouse? What kinds of things are helpful to know in advance, before tragedy strikes?

First, be aware of the fact that as personal stress increases, so does stress on a relationship. Simply knowing this can help you get through the tough times, enabling you to "tread water" for a while until the stress eases. One couple, whose child was hospitalized for a serious injury, was told by my husband, "Be prepared for some tension in your marriage." Later, as the two found themselves in a heated religious argument, they recalled Eric's words. Just knowing that what was happening to them was normal and strongly related to the anxiety they were feeling over their son helped them through a stormy time in their relationship.

Second, when both of you are at a low ebb, look to outside help for emotional support. You simply cannot give what you don't have. Lana, a young mother of two girls, fell asleep on the couch one evening as she waited for her husband to return home from a business trip. She was awakened by thick smoke. She immediately fell to the floor and attempted to crawl to her daughters' room and remove them from the inferno. Totally overcome by smoke, she turned and crawled for the outside door, hoping to fill her lungs with clear air and return for the girls. However, she was unable to reenter the building. The two children perished in the fire. The guilt and agony that Lana experienced was equaled only by the sense of helplessness and despair felt by her husband. The two turned all their pain toward each other, and when their needs were not met, sorrow became bitterness and bitterness became hostility. Within a year after the crisis the marriage was dissolved.

Third, if a crisis occurs that primarily affects your spouse (the death of his parent, for example), allow him the time and space to grieve. Often people are so uncomfortable with the expression of grief that they attempt to stop up the flow of emotions with a religious euphemism. I remember one well-meaning Christian who came to the funeral of a woman in our church who had died suddenly of a heart attack. Meeting the woman's husband at the door, she extended her hand in sympathy, saying, "I'm sure God had a reason for this."

"If He did," the man responded, "it will be a long time before I understand it."

It simply isn't fair to try to pretend that all is right with the world when it is not. And pat sayings that shut off emotion only serve to prevent a person from working through grief. Psychologists recognize several stages of grief that an individual passes through when dealing with tragedy. It is helpful to be aware of these when someone close to you is bereaved.

1. The initial reaction is one of disbelief, followed by shock and numbness.

2. Once the initial shock wears off, a person begins to express emotion. It is crucial that an individual be allowed to express this agony.

3. Several symptoms of distress can then appear:
   a. depression
   b. physical reactions
   c. guilt

    d. hostility

    e. inability to function normally

  4. Gradually hope is restored.

  5. The individual readjusts to life.[4]

Fourth, if the crisis involves a spouse bottoming out because of alcohol, remember the advice of Alcoholics Anonymous. Al-Anon suggests that the spouse of a drinking alcoholic can help himself or herself and the children by "releasing" the spouse emotionally. Interestingly, some of Al-Anon's principles can also be applied to someone extremely spiritual whose spouse has no interest in religion. The "releasing" process is done by:

  1. Surrendering the obsessive and futile attempt to control the spouse's drinking—[or religious life].

  2. Giving up the many ways in which the person has stood between the spouse and the natural consequences of his or her irresponsible behavior.

  3. Abandoning the assumption that all improvement in the situation depends entirely on whether or not the spouse stops drinking—[or becomes converted].

  4. Developing a more fulfilling life for himself or herself and the children, regardless of what the alcoholic [or non-Christian spouse] decides to do.[5]

Last of all, cement your relationship now, so that when a crisis does occur, you are better prepared to handle it. In *Nobody's Boy* I tell the story of my parents' search for religious meaning in life. When my father first found the answers to questions he had battled with all his life, he was eager to share his newfound faith. But my mother was not ready to listen to what he had to say. Too many other factors prevented her religious interest at that time. Ten years later, however, when her own mother passed away, she became consumed by grief. Watching her agony, my father was touched by the feeling of her pain. Acting out of his love for her, and on the basis of a solid relationship already established, he began to share with her the hope that he found in the Bible. The time was right. She listened. Comforted, she later accepted his beliefs. In her own words, from *Nobody's Boy:* "You helped me a lot when you talked to me about death that evening, Jim. Your words soothed me, calmed my crying nerves. And afterward, when the pain had waned into numbness, the words were still there, appealing to my mind." [6]

People do not wish a crisis upon themselves or their families. But at times, in the midst of suffering, new truths can be perceived and new strength gained. At such times we are given the opportunity to help each other in ways that may never again be possible.

Notes

[1] Howard J. Clinebell, Jr., *Basic Types of Pastoral Care and Counseling* (Nashville: Abingdon, 1966), p. 160.

[2] Gruzen, *Raising Your Jewish-Christian Child,* p. 161.

[3] Joy Swift, *They're All Dead, Aren't They?* (Boise, Idaho: Pacific Press, 1986), p. 188.

[4] Robert W. Bailey, *Stages of Grief* (Grand Rapids: Zondervan, 1976), pp. 79-81.

[5] Clinebell, p. 173.

[6] Sandra Doran, *Nobody's Boy* (Washington, D.C.: Review and Herald, 1982), p. 82.

Conversion:
The Ultimate Goal?

9

"Mr. Adams, are you ready for Jesus to come?" My husband's voice, raised to a loud pitch, reverberated off the hospital walls, bouncing down the sterile corridor and sounding in my ears as I waited in the empty lobby.

"Mr. Adams . . ." Once again the insistent question sounded, the decibels higher yet, the enunciation clearer still to counter the old man's deafness.

A nurse padded by noiselessly, and I noted more sharply the contrast between the hushed environment and Eric's stentorian voice.

I stood up quickly and made my way down the gray-and-white hallway, past interns, carts of linens and IVs, and slightly ajar doors. I stopped at the last room on the left and paused in the doorway, surveying the scene within.

A woman sat in the red vinyl chair by the window, her hands mechanically clutching the straps of a worn black purse. In the bed to her right lay a man propped up with two pillows, his white hair long and unruly, his blue eyes blazing with a power that formed a startling contrast to the weakened frame that housed him.

To the right of the bed stood my husband, bending close over the rugged profile, holding both of the old gentleman's hands in his own, still pleading for a simple response.

As I watched, a change flashed over the old man's face, almost imperceptible at first, but lingering, and settling over the eyes of fire, softening the countenance, putting to rest some hotly raging controversy within. The old man said nothing, yet the relaxing of his visage suggested something stronger than any amount of words could have possibly conveyed.

Eric, aware, stopped talking. For a brief moment the room became still, caught, it seemed, between the spinning of two worlds. But the woman by the window had not sensed the nuance of a look, the subtlety of perception. In an instant she was standing by the bedside, assuming the role she had played for the past 50 years.

"John," she began, "you've got to give your life to Jesus. All these years I've been begging with you, pleading with you to throw away the cigarettes, stop the card games, the drinking, the swearing . . ."

The moment was gone. His craggy profile hardening back into the lines etched over a half-century of marriage, John turned and faced the other side of the room in stony silence. If religion meant submission to the dictates of this woman who had tried to play conscience to him for five decades, if it meant the satisfaction of an "I told you so" blazing in righteous features across her face, if it meant admitting that every argument, disagreement, and fight had been his fault as a "non-Christian," then he would have no part of it.

Two months later I sat in a small chapel, listening to the dripping of rain from the eaves, tapping a steady pattered-background while Eric's voice lifted in solemn tones above a plain brown casket. "John Adams passed to his rest on the twenty-fourth day of October . . ." he began.

In the front row sat a woman, clutching in one hand a worn black purse and in the other a small moist handkerchief. As the sermon came to a close, she could bear it no longer. Bowing her head, she let them flow, the tears of 50 years of marriage, of desperately fighting for the soul of another, of always hoping, ever praying, and never winning. The battle was over, and he was no closer to home. Taking the arm of a friend, she summoned the dignity to rise, then made her way slowly out of the church and to the waiting limousine.

Converting one's spouse. To some the issue is a lifelong battle, the stuff of which every argument is made, the very purpose for existence. Doggedly, such husbands and wives persist in a relationship, progressing only in their increased determination to "win."

And while such a power struggle may seem a bit extreme, it is often present under the surface, to greater or lesser degrees, when spouses do not share the same religious convictions.

The desire to convert one's spouse can actually spring from a number of motives, not all as pure as one might wish to believe. While it is natural to want to share something as significant as religious beliefs with one close to you, there are a host of "hidden agendas" that tend to cluster around the simple desire to convince your spouse of your beliefs. And such agendas are present not only when a person attempts to convert a spouse to his or her own religion, but also, conversely, when a person wishes to dissuade a spouse of his or her religious convictions.

If you desire that your spouse change his or her religious outlook, think about it for a moment. What are the underlying reasons for your wish?

One woman, who spent 25 years of marriage with an "unconverted husband," had an ironic story to tell me. For 25 years she had lived for the day when her husband would join her faith, making her family united spiritually. Yet when her dream became reality, she suddenly realized that after the initial elation, she felt let down.

"It's taken me awhile to realize that during all those years I pinned everything on Gary's conversion. It was the panacea for all my troubles. If only Gary were converted, our marriage would be better . . . the kids would listen to me . . . we'd argue less. And now that it's happened, I find that my paper tiger has been destroyed. There is nothing to blame all my marriage trouble on now.

"Any relationship takes work. It was too easy, I guess, to pin everything on Gary. My desire for his conversion actually sprang from selfish motives. I wanted *my* life to be easier. I wanted to be married to this self-effacing person who would always treat me gently, kindly. Who wouldn't want that? But Christianity doesn't guarantee instant perfection . . . not on my part, not on his."

This woman found out the hard way that when the deeper issues of marriage are not dealt with, they will not instantly resolve themselves upon the conversion of a spouse. And as wistfully as one might look upon Christian couples, all is not bliss after the car pulls out of the church parking lot at noon. A friend of mine, married to a non-Christian, once remarked, "I find it good medicine, once in a while, to hear that Christian marriages have their problems too. So often I fantasize and think that Christian marriages are perfect. But they're not, and when Christian couples can be honest about that, I find myself better able to appreciate my own husband."

So converting one's spouse will not guarantee marital bliss. Neither will it guarantee that the individual you are yoked with will mirror all your opinions and ideas.

There is a human tendency to identify ourselves so fully with those we love, psychologists tell us, that we look at them as accretions to ourselves. In other words, we allow our self-concept to be tied in not only to who we are, but also to the identity of those close to us.

As a Christian, do you view your spouse as an embarrassing extension of yourself, as part of your identity that draws negative attention? Do you feel as if "your slip is showing" being married to one who is not converted? If there is an element of this present, you might find it difficult to release your spouse emotionally, even if he or she did convert to your religion. There will always be something said or done that is not exactly as you would feel comfortable having it said or done.

One reserved husband I know has spent virtually his whole marriage trying to make over his Brooklyn-bred wife, who is the life of the party. He sees her as an extension of himself—one that he finds awkward and embarrassing.

Another more subtle motive for attempting to convert one's spouse has to do with the roles we play as husband and wife. An earlier chapter dealt with the concept of transactional analysis—the taking on of adult, parent, or child roles. In taking such roles, there is another hat that is sometimes worn by an individual—that of the messiah. We've all met individuals who think of themselves as self-styled saviors, who can't function unless they are in the role of helper while everyone around them must be troubled and in need of help.

Certainly the majority of husbands and wives whose religious interests differ do not fall into this category. Perhaps there has been some accusation on the part of one spouse that the other is "playing God," but this can spring from personal guilt rather than genuine perception. But it might be helpful to honestly ask yourself the question Is it possible that there is an element of "the messiah" present in my relationships with others and, particularly, with my spouse? If so, what are the implications for myself, for my spouse?

Carmen Berry, a social worker who found herself driven to help others on the job and through a myriad of volunteer positions at her church, realized suddenly that she was burned out. Finding that her situation was not uncommon, she wrote the book *When Helping You Is Hurting Me: Escaping the Messiah Trap*. Describing the pattern, she says this: "Messiahs neglect themselves because they feel that they are supposed to sacrifice their own well-being for the sake of others. This is the messiah definition of love. . . . [It] is an odd combination of feeling grandiose yet worthless, of being needed and yet abandoned, of playing God while groveling."

She goes on: "In my background the church overemphasized helping others to the neglect of one's own growth. There is a heavy emphasis on helping other people without struggling with what it means to really love people." [1]

"By promoting themselves as superhuman beings, [messiahs] avoid real intimacy." [2]

And therein lies the problem. When one person sets himself or herself up as the one who is always in control, never in need of help, undaunted, indispensable—it becomes impossible for another to love him or her as an honest and vulnerable human being. Relationships that are based on the idea "You'll be OK once I help you out" are dangerously unbalanced. Spouses who will accept a partner only after he or she can help them relinquish the "crutch of religion" are just as unfair as the one who will accept his or her spouse as soon as he or she converts.

Something doesn't ring quite clear when we go about our affairs with the intention of effecting a change in another person. C. S. Lewis suggests that it is much easier to live with "ordinary people who get over their tantrums . . . unemphatically, letting a meal, a night's sleep, or a joke mend all" than with those who "make every trifle a matter of explicitly spiritual importance." [3]

Like the proverbial butterfly, which lands only on those who do not pursue it, conversion is an effect rather than a cause. It is not something one does *to* or *for* someone else, but rather, something that comes, if at all, when eager hands are not there to grasp at its wings and present it to another.

Of all the stories that might be used to illustrate this point, I find that of a humble, elderly man in our first church the most impressive. At the age of 65, Don became a Christian, focusing all the energies of his retirement years into a small white church and the needs of its congregation. Lou, his wife of many years, was pleased to see her husband involved in something that so obviously lifted his spirits, yet she did not share the same religious interest and convictions.

Five years after his conversion, Don discovered that he had cancer. Methodically he put his affairs in order. Carefully he arranged his bank accounts so that his wife could pick up the books with no confusion. He called painters, plumbers, and carpenters to do all the small repairs needed around the house. He spent hours reflecting on his life and placed several phone calls, making things right with those he had slighted. And through all of this, Lou moved in a haze, unable to accept what was happening to her husband.

When it was finally over, Lou returned to her home, empty, alone, sick at heart. But something of Don remained with her. She took comfort from the stability of his life, the strength of his faith. And that butterfly, whose wings he had been careful not to tear, gently lighted upon her shoulder. For it was to the small white church that she ultimately turned for answers and renewed hope. And the religion that Don never forced upon his wife gave new meaning to her existence.

Is conversion, then, the ultimate goal in marriages between individuals whose religious outlooks differ? Had Don believed that, the last five years of his life and marriage would have been a time of tension and divisiveness rather than a period of increased strength and unity. And who is to say what his wife would have turned to after the end?

Notes

[1] Carmen Berry, in Jim and Phyllis Alsdurf, "False Messiahs," *Christianity Today*, Dec. 9, 1988, p. 35.

[2] Alsdurf, p. 35.

[3] C. S. Lewis, *The Four Loves* (New York: Harcourt Brace, 1960), p. 185.

Clarifying:
Putting Things Into
Perspective

10

God grant me the serenity to accept the things I
cannot change, the courage to change the things I
can, and the wisdom to know the difference."

In a marriage where religion is not a shared experience, such words take on a special significance.

Accept. What needs to be accepted as an individual
married to one whose basic philosophy of life does not
parallel my own?

*I should accept the fact that the difference of reli-
gious commitment is no easier for my spouse than it is
for me.* How often we look at things from our own
perspective, forgetting that our spouse is struggling
with the same issues! Says one Christian: "The one time
I finally got my husband to come to church with me, he
wore his sunglasses through the entire service. And
suddenly I realized . . . the same awkwardness that I
experience every time he asks me to an office party . . .
the same uncomfortable 'out-of-my-element' feeling
that crops up every time we are around his friends,
Rodney feels when he's around mine. This whole thing
is no easier for him than it is for me."

*I should accept the fact that every marriage has its
challenges, whether both spouses are Christians or not.*
These words from Patti Roberts, ex-wife of evangelist
Richard Roberts (Oral Roberts' son), express the reality

that even on high levels of religious involvement problems persist.

"I'm not divorcing just Richard, but a whole realm that puts religious achievement and lifestyle above sanctity of life. I'm divorcing the end-justifies-the-means theory. I'm divorcing the belief that products are more important than people. I'm divorcing the god of family image. . . . I'm divorcing the preference for public prayers over private penitence. I'm divorcing the person who had never learned that 'a man shall leave his father and mother, and the two shall become one.' . . . I'm divorcing the mentality that caused the last act of this marriage to be handled with the publicity value in mind. Oh, dear God, help me to the other side." [1]

I should accept the fact that ultimately each person is responsible for his or her own decisions. I have not been given the privilege of living your life for you, nor have you mine. The best I can do is to affirm your personhood, offer the support and acceptance that will best enable you to grow as an individual.

I should accept the fact that there will always be pluses and minuses in every relationship and resolve to focus on the pluses. In an article entitled "Happily Ever After, Indeed!" Trish Vradenburg speaks of the third stage of marriage, in which you "come to terms with your marriage and why it's worth the ups and downs." "What saves the relationship," she says, "is that your plus column is fuller than your minus column. Maybe he doesn't tell you how incredible you look when you've spent three hours putting yourself together (minus), but he unloads the dishwasher without being asked (plus). Although he doesn't surprise you with tickets for a weekend in Miami (small minus), he treats both you and your parents with respect (big plus)." [2]

The point is that you can always find the negatives if you look for them, but the positives are there too.

I should accept the fact that working at a marriage is much easier than terminating one. Pat Conroy, reflecting on his own divorce in an article that appeared in *Atlanta* magazine, makes this point in poignant terms: "I find it hard to believe how many people now get divorced, how many submit to such extraordinary pain. For there are no clean divorces. Divorces should be conducted in [slaughterhouses] or surgical wards. In my own case, I think it would have been easier if Barbara had died. I would have been gallant at her funeral and shed real tears—far easier than staring across a table, telling each other it was over.

"It was a killing thing to look at the mother of my children and know that we would not be together for the rest of our lives. It was terrifying to say goodbye, to reject a part of my own history." [3]

Terminating a marriage relationship is like unweaving a thick rope fiber by fiber. The process is painful, and when you are finished, you are left with nothing more than a shapeless mass of straw. It is far easier to put one's energy into repairing the torn strands than unraveling the whole mass.

God grant me the serenity to accept the things I cannot change, the courage to change the things I can . . . What things can be changed, as I look at my relationship as it stands now?

I can change the stereotype I have hidden behind in classifying my marriage. The support group of Christian women with nonbelieving husbands I met with has an admirable list of goals, which they review at the beginning of each session. These women strive to:

1. stop complaining about their husbands.
2. realize that there are no pat answers.
3. lose the identity of "me with the unsaved husband."

Such goals are certainly worthy of pursuit. The third

one, particularly, emphasizes the need of breaking out of a stereotype, and relating to one's spouse on a higher level than that of a "symbol."

I can change the mind-set that puts me in charge of my spouse's religious decisions. As one Lutheran woman remarked to me: "My husband has no interest in joining a church himself, and I wouldn't even try to meddle in that area of his life. He was brought up Baptist. He knows what it's all about. He's an adult. He can decide what he wants to do."

I can change the tendency of "postponing" marital happiness until some future time when my spouse converts to my religious outlook. The antithesis of this point is expressed by one woman who remarked to a friend, "If I knew now that my husband would never convert to my religion, I would leave him without a backward look. The only thing that keeps me hanging on is the hope that someday he will change."

What a tragic way to experience a marriage! Such an attitude will surely not hasten the desired goal, and if by chance this woman's husband does convert, what a fragmented marriage the two will be left to deal with!

I can change the attitude that my way of looking at things is right and that I can gain nothing from listening to my spouse. Says Herbert H. Lehman, businessman and former United States senator, "No individual and no nation has a monopoly of wisdom or talent. When an individual or a nation becomes self-satisfied or complacent, it is time, I believe, to be deeply concerned. He who closes his ears to the views of others shows little confidence in the integrity of his own views."[4]

I can change any image I might have constructed of my spouse that shows a lack of respect. In speaking of insuring success in a business, Thomas Watson, Jr., says in *A Business and Its Beliefs,* "IBM's philosophy is largely contained in three simple beliefs. I want to begin with what I think is the most important: *our respect for the individual*. This is a simple concept, but in IBM it occupies a major portion of management time. We devote more effort to it than anything else." [5]

If a business finds respect of the individual crucial to its operation, how much more important must it be to something as significant as a marriage! And notice that IBM cites two things necessary to insure the respect of the individual: time and effort. Respect does not always flow automatically; it is something that must be worked on.

Serenity to accept. Courage to change. And then comes that illusive gray area: ". . . and the wisdom to know the difference." In each marriage there are nuances, subtleties, patterns that defy universality. These are the areas that drain the dregs of our emotional reserves, tax us mentally, exhaust us physically. Yet each decision that is made, each moment of time that is dedicated to "working it out," lifts the haze of gray a bit more, brightens the outlook of our marriage.

It is not easy, this marriage between individuals whose religious outlooks are as different as a Christmas creche and a bottle of champagne. But anything that requires extra work takes on extra value, for there is something highly treasured about that which is not easily obtained.

Notes

[1] Patti Roberts and Sherry Andrews, *Ashes to Gold* (Waco, Tex.: Word Books, 1983), p. 22.

[2] Trish Vradenburg, "Happily Ever After, Indeed!" *Woman's Day*, Sept. 1, 1987.

[3] Pat Conroy, "Death of a Marriage." *Atlanta*, November 1978.

[4] In Edward Murrow, *This I Believe* (New York: Simon and Schuster, 1952), pp. 99, 100.

[5] In Thomas J. Peters and Robert H. Waterman, Jr., *In Search of Excellence* (New York: Warner Books, 1982), p. 238.

Enjoy an Even Better Marriage With Nancy Van Pelt's Books and Cassettes

The Compleat Marriage
Nancy Van Pelt combines psychological insights with biblical principles to show how any couple can have the compleat marriage. You will learn how to understand, fulfill, communicate with, and have a balanced relationship with your mate. Paper, 175 pages. US$9.50, Cdn$11.90.

The Compleat Marriage Cassettes
Pop these cassettes into your car deck or pocket stereo and continue your active lifestyle while learning the principles of a satisfying marriage. Binder and four cassettes (average length 40 minutes each side). US$14.95, Cdn$18.70.

The Compleat Marriage Workbook
This married couples' guide to acceptance, communication, and love provides additional material and tests for self-evaluation. Paper, 76 pages. US$5.95, Cdn$7.45.

About the author:
Nancy Van Pelt has been featured on numerous radio and television shows, covering many facets of courtship, marriage, human sexuality, and parenting. She and her husband teach Compleat Parent and Compleat Marriage seminars based on the books she has authored.

To order, call **1-800-765-6955** or write to ABC Mailing Service, P.O. Box 1119, Hagerstown, MD 21741. Send check or money order. Enclose applicable sales tax and 15 percent (minimum US$2.50) for postage and handling. Prices and availability subject to change without notice. Add 7 percent GST in Canada.

Inspiration and Practical Help for Growing Christians

In Pastures Green
In 1975 Bev Condy left the rush of city life and took up farming
in the Sierra Nevada foothills. Her stubborn, silly sheep, along
with horses, cats, geese, goats, a stray dog, and friendly
neighbors, gave her insights into human nature and God's love.
Paper, 96 pages. US$6.95, Cdn$8.70.

Hurt, Healing, and Happy Again
Life hurts. The 15 people in this book can prove it by their
firsthand experiences. But as they hurt, they made beautiful
discoveries about God's providence. Martin Weber's inspiring
book is filled with their triumphant stories and will bring you
assurance of God's personal involvement in your own life. Paper,
160 pages. US$2.50, Cdn$3.15.

The Making of a Mother
Karen Spruill shares the personal learning process that set her
free from feelings of loneliness, frustration, and inadequacy. She
also offers practical advice on breast feeding, toilet training,
money matters, and discipline. Paper, 128 pages. US$7.95,
Cdn$9.95.

Time Out for Moms
Cheryl Woolsey Holloway's devotional book for young mothers
bubbles over with honesty, warmth, and sparkling humor.
Mothers will find encouragement and strength and enjoy the rare
luxury of being nurtured. Paper, 94 pages. US$6.95, Cdn$8.70.

To order, call **1-800-765-6955** or write to ABC Mailing Service, P.O. Box
1119, Hagerstown, MD 21741. Send check or money order. Enclose
applicable sales tax and 15 percent (minimum US$2.50) for postage and
handling. Prices and availability subject to change without notice. Add 7
percent GST in Canada.